A Library of Modern Religious Thought

S. T. COLERIDGE
Confessions of an Inquiring Spirit

A LIBRARY OF
MODERN RELIGIOUS THOUGHT

General Editor: Henry Chadwick

SAMUEL TAYLOR COLERIDGE

CONFESSIONS OF
AN INQUIRING SPIRIT

Reprinted from the third edition 1853
with the introduction by Joseph Henry Green
and the note by Sara Coleridge

EDITED WITH AN INTRODUCTORY NOTE BY
H. STJ. HART, B.D.
FELLOW AND DEAN OF QUEENS' COLLEGE, CAMBRIDGE

ADAM & CHARLES BLACK
LONDON

THIS EDITION FIRST PUBLISHED 1956
A. AND C. BLACK LTD.
4, 5 AND 6 SOHO SQUARE, LONDON, W.I

MADE IN GREAT BRITAIN
PRINTED BY WILLIAM CLOWES AND SONS, LTD
LONDON AND BECCLES

CONTENTS

INTRODUCTORY NOTE

Samuel Taylor Coleridge, poet, philosopher, polymath, and talker, was born on 21 October 1772 in his father's parsonage at Ottery St. Mary, and died in the house of the Gillmans in Highgate on 25 July 1834. In his *Confessions of an Inquiring Spirit,* which is here reprinted, he has, as he tells us,[1] delivered his "entire mind" on the "momentous Question" of the inspiration of the Christian Scriptures. The book is cast in the form of seven letters to a friend, and the reader will do well to suppose that friend to be himself. The letters concern "the bounds between the right, and the superstitious, use and estimation of the Sacred Canon."[2] In them Coleridge anticipated positions which others were only to reach after decades of controversy, and a recent writer has pointed out that if more attention had been paid to Coleridge much of that controversy, which was often at once unhappy and unedifying, might have been spared.[3]

The book was first printed from the Author's manuscript by Henry Nelson Coleridge in 1840. A second edition in 1849,[4] with an "Advertisement," or introductory note, by Sara Coleridge, added an Introduction by Joseph Henry Green, which examines Coleridge's indebtedness to Lessing,[5] a long "Note on the Confessions of an Inquiring

---

[1] Below, p. 80.

[2] Below, p. 38.

[3] Professor Basil Willey, *Nineteenth Century Studies, Coleridge to Matthew Arnold,* p. 40: "The standpoint of the Letters transcends the level of the later Science-and-Religion controversies, none of which need have arisen had his ground been firmly occupied from the beginning."

[4] The first and the second editions were both printed by William Pickering. For details see T. J. Wise, *A Bibliography of the Writings in Prose and Verse of Samuel Taylor Coleridge,* London, 1913, pp. 162 ff.

[5] Green need not have been quite so anxious in his defence of Coleridge, at all events in one particular, namely Coleridge's use of the word "Bibliolatry," (below, pp. 29, 58 and 77). It was already an English word. The earliest instance cited by the *O.E.D.* is from John Byrom, who died in 1763. There are two passages in which Byrom uses the word; both are in poetry of a kind. The former, from the third of his *Familiar Epistles to a Friend,* reads: "In ev'ry Way that Words and Sense agree,/ 'Tis perfect Bibliolatry to me." The latter, from *A Stricture on the Rev. Mr. Warburton's Doctrine of Grace,* reads: "If to adore an Image be Idolatry/ To deify a Book is Bibliolatry." See *Miscellaneous Poems* by

7

Spirit" by Sara Coleridge, in which Coleridge is defended from criticisms which had been made in an article entitled "Tendencies toward the Subversion of Faith" which had appeared in the *English Review* for December 1848, and some other pieces by Coleridge himself. The third edition in 1853, with an "Advertisement" by Derwent Coleridge, retained the Introduction by Green, and the Note by Sara Coleridge, but omitted the additional pieces by Coleridge himself. The fourth edition in 1863 was a reprint of the third edition.[1] In 1884 the *Confessions of an Inquiring Spirit* was appended to the Bohn text of the *Aids to Reflection.*

The present reprint is from a copy of the third edition, of 1853, though the table of contents has been modelled on that of the second edition, of 1849. We thus reprint both Green's Introduction[2] and Sara Coleridge's long Note. These are both period pieces of some tediousness. But those who to-day read the *Confessions* will either be chiefly interested in Coleridge or in the religious thought of the nineteenth century. For the former interest Green's Introduction, for the latter both Green's Introduction and Sara Coleridge's Note, are documents of importance which it will be convenient to have at hand. The reader will find them instructive both for what they say and for the way in which they say it. It is not easy to suppose that they are likely to be reprinted again.

The Bohn edition of 1884, by printing the *Confessions* after the *Aids to Reflection,* put the *Confessions* into the right company. For the *Confessions* is one of six "Disquisitions Supplemental of the Aids to Reflection" which Coleridge planned[3]—perhaps the only one which he in fact succeeded in writing. We may read of the plan in a letter from Coleridge to Mr. Hessey, of the year 1825, in which Coleridge speaks of his six disquisitions, and the sixth of them is to be "On the right and

John Byrom, Manchester, 1773, vol. 2, pp. 125 and 331, or the edition of Leeds, 1814, vol. 2, pp. 79 and 210. Coleridge will also have read the word in Lessing. It is just such a word as Coleridge would have liked to have invented himself, and wherever he first met it or heard it, he is not likely to have allowed it to go from his vocabulary. For Lessing on "Bibliolatrie" see *Schriften,* edited Lachmann and Muncker, vol. xvi (1902), pp. 470 ff.

[1] The third and fourth editions were printed by Edward Moxon. Details in Wise, *loc. cit.*

[2] See note 5 on pages 7–8.

[3] See E. K. Chambers, *Samuel Taylor Coleridge, A Biographical Study,* Oxford, 1938, p. 311.

superstitious Use and Estimation of the Scriptures."[1] Another letter,[2] of 23 May 1825, to the same, discusses the general plan and *mould* of the proposed disquisitions, suggesting a different and delightful title. Coleridge was a past master of writing prospectuses of books which he never was in the end to write, as he himself knew very well. The plan contained in this letter is an excellent example of this kind of writing, and although there is no direct reference in it to the book which subsequently appeared as the *Confessions of an Inquiring Spirit*, the reader will find it convenient to be able to refer to it. It has therefore been added at the end of the volume.[3]

The proper appraisal of the *Confessions*[4] belongs accordingly with that of the *Aids to Reflection*, of which the present publishers have an annotated reprint in mind. The influence of Coleridge in keeping within the Church of England scholars who were disturbed by the controversies of the early and middle nineteenth century was acknowledged at the time, and has since been studied.[5] Coleridge, the anticipator, seemed to have seen all the problems in advance, and in advance he seemed to many to have provided his church with a satisfying apologetic, reconciling Christianity with modern thought. Naturally we find that contemporary acknowledgement is to Coleridge in general, or to the *Aids to Reflection*, rather than to these supplementary *Confessions*, which are limited to the discussion of the use and estimation of the Scriptures. It was not until the end of the nineteenth century and the beginning of this that the kind of position for which Coleridge argued in the *Confessions* was at all widely held inside the churches,[6] and then perhaps only for a short time,[7] and perhaps with little idea that Coleridge was the father of such views.[8] He had anticipated later

[1] E. L. Griggs, *Unpublished Letters of Samuel Taylor Coleridge*, London, 1932, letter 348.   [2] Griggs, *ibid.*, letter 352.   [3] Below, p. 119.

[4] For the best modern discussion see Willey, *op. cit.*, pp. 38–44.

[5] See especially Charles Richard Sanders, *Coleridge and the Broad Church Movement*, Durham, North Carolina, Duke University Press, 1942.

[6] After reading the *Confessions* it is instructive to turn to the section on Scripture, pp. 27–35, of the Report of the Commission on Christian Doctrine appointed by the Archbishops of Canterbury and York, published under the title *Doctrine in the Church of England*, 1938 (S.P.C.K.).

[7] Note that the Commission on Doctrine (foregoing note) was appointed in 1922.

[8] The article in the *Harvard Theological Review*, vol. xi, January 1918, by Herbert L. Stewart, entitled "The Place of Coleridge in English Theology," recognizes this (*ibid.*, pp. 18 ff.).

developments. To-day we are already able to look back on those developments, and very soon the pundits will be delivering their verdicts upon them. In the meantime the *Confessions of an Inquiring Spirit* remains an important text for students of religious thought in England in the nineteenth century, and the distinguished Coleridgean scholar Professor Kathleen Coburn has recently reminded us[1] that it has long been out of print. Here accordingly it is.[2]

H. St̲J. H.

[1] Kathleen Coburn, *Inquiring Spirit, A New Presentation of Coleridge from his Published and Unpublished Prose Writings*, London, 1951, p. 22.

[2] "The book is like refined Gold; its value is great, though its bulk be little." Quoted from *The Morning Post*, in an advertisement (1849) of the *Confessions*.

ADVERTISEMENT TO THE FIRST EDITION

The following Letters on the Inspiration of the Scriptures were left by Mr. Coleridge in MS. at his death. The Reader will find in them a key to most of the Biblical criticism scattered throughout the Author's own writings, and an affectionate, pious, and, as the Editor humbly believes, a profoundly wise attempt to place the study of the Written Word on its only sure foundation,—a deep sense of God's holiness and truth, and a consequent reverence for that Light—the image of Himself—which He has kindled in every one of his rational creatures.—H. N. C.

LINCOLN'S INN,
   September 22 1840

ADVERTISEMENT TO THE SECOND EDITION

The following Introduction was composed by Mr. Green in consequence of my consulting him on the subject of my Father's obligations to Lessing in the *Confessions of an Inquiring Spirit,* and was intended by him to be used as materials for a preface to this new edition of the work. As it appears however to require no remodelling, either by omission or addition, I present it just as it came from the author's pen.—S.C. 1849.

ADVERTISEMENT TO THE THIRD EDITION

The present edition of the *Confessions of an Inquiring Spirit* differs from the last, only by the removal of some miscellaneous pieces, which appeared to take from the unity without adding to the completeness of the work. These will appear in their proper places in a forthcoming volume. The Introduction by Mr. Green, and the defence of the Author's views by his lamented daughter, will still be read with interest.—D.C.

St. Mark's College, Chelsea,
   April, 1853

A MANUSCRIPT OF
THE CONFESSIONS OF AN INQUIRING SPIRIT

There is a manuscript of the Confessions of an Inquiring Spirit in the British Museum, which by the kindness of the authorities I have been allowed to inspect. It is listed in the *Catalogue of Additions to the MSS. in the British Museum MDCCCLXXXVIII–MDCCCXCIII,* and is item 15 in Add. MS. 34,225. In the catalogue it is very justly described as 'probably an early draft, with many slight variations from the printed edition.'

CONFESSIONS OF AN INQUIRING SPIRIT

Faith subsists in the *synthesis* of the Reason and the individual Will. By virtue of the latter it must be an energy, and, inasmuch as it relates to the whole moral man, it must be exerted in each and all of his constituents or incidents, faculties and tendencies:—it must be a total, not a partial—a continuous, not a desultory or occasional—energy. And by virtue of the former, that is, Reason, Faith must be a Light, a form of knowing, a beholding of Truth. In the incomparable words of the Evangelist, therefore,—*Faith must be a Light originating in the Logos, or the substantial Reason, which is coeternal and one with the Holy Will, and which Light is at the same time the Life of men.* Now as *Life* is here the sum or collective of all moral and spiritual acts, in suffering, doing, and being, so is Faith the source and the sum, the energy and the principle of the fidelity of Man to God, by the subordination of his human Will, in all provinces of his nature, to his Reason, as the sum of spiritual Truth, representing and manifesting the Will Divine.—*Literary Remains,* vol. iv, p. 437.

INTRODUCTION

BY JOSEPH HENRY GREEN, ESQ.

In preparing a new edition of this work, it is scarcely less than a duty to its revered Author to draw the attention of the reader to the theological writings of Lessing, in order to obviate any mistake, similar to that which has been already made, with regard to the Author's originality, or at all events to exhibit, without reserve, the grounds upon which a charge of plagiarism might possibly be founded. It will be discovered, namely, on a comparison of this essay with certain works of the German writer, that there exists so marked a similarity of opinion on some points of doctrine, that the reader might be inclined to adopt, as the most obvious explanation of the resemblance, the supposition that Coleridge had not only derived the advantage, which every writer is likely to do from the acumen and labours of a predecessor, but that he had transferred without acknowledgment Lessing's thoughts to his own pages; nor will the supposition want the support derived from the capability of tracing here and there similar language, if not identical phrases. Nay, it cannot be denied that Coleridge was a student of Lessing's writings; since, in a fly-leaf of one of the volumes of a copy of his works, which belonged to Coleridge, the latter says: "Year after year I have made a point of re-perusing the *Kleine Schriften* as masterpieces of style and argument."

Notwithstanding these admissions, it may be reasonably doubted, however, that any candid person, after the perusal of Lessing's works here in question, and a careful collation of them with the "Confessions," would venture to assume that Coleridge had forfeited his claim to originality in the view which he has here taken of "the bounds between the right and the superstitious use and estimation of the Sacred Canon:" and it may far rather be anticipated that the result of such comparison would be the conviction that, whatever portions of the "Confessions" may be justly ascribed to Lessing, they were no less the growths and natural educts of the different and deeper principle out of which Coleridge's scheme of theology had shaped itself. It is

2   17

indeed highly probable that Coleridge had received a lasting impression from the perusal of the *Kleine Schriften,* and that when engaged in producing a work, the tendency of which was in some respects similar, the recollections of those writings would blend with his own thoughts, and lead him to adopt similar arguments, and even in some instances the same expressions. It is true that no reference is anywhere made to the German author; but when we consider that the "Confessions" were written with an object, which can scarcely be said to have anything in common with Lessing's controversial essays, and were the result of a different process of reasoning, which presented only insulated points of contact with Lessing's arguments, it will not surprise us if the reminiscences in question did not become objects of conscious remembrance. For Coleridge, truth was impersonal; and if he adopted from others, it was because it was alien to the habit of his mind to consider the perception or discovery of truth as any thing which belonged exclusively and appropriately to the individual. He was ever ready to assist others in the elaboration of their thoughts, and ever reckoned as little of the rights of his own intellectual proprietorship as if truth and knowledge were the same common property as light and air.

That the correspondences and resemblances, to which we have above adverted, and which after all do not amount to much, afford any just ground for impugning the originality of Coleridge may be safely denied. In the case of a work, which is an aggregate and not a growth, in which by eclectic ingenuity

> "Purpureus, latè qui splendeat, unus et alter
> Assuitur pannus;"—Horace, *A. P.,* l. 15,

it would be as just to reclaim, as it would be easy to detach, the borrowed fragments: but where the work is the result of a formative principle which gives it unity and totality, where the thoughts and reasonings are the development of a living principle to an organic whole, it may be safely assumed that the author who interweaves with his own the kindred products of other men's minds, is impelled only by the sense and pleasurable sympathy of a common intellectual activity, and that he would, or might have arrived at the same or similar results, where these are potentially contained in the principle, which gave birth to his reasonings. That Coleridge's theology was the growth of his own mind, and inseparably united with his philosophy, it is not here the place to exhibit. Nor indeed is it necessary for our present purpose, that of considering any supposed, or hitherto unacknowledged intellectual debts to Lessing. And it may be preliminarily observed that if the reader, conversant with German, after reading Lessing's theological writings, including his philosophical essay on the Trinity, and the fragment entitled *Erziehung des Menschengeschlechts*, will thoughtfully peruse the "Confessions," especially the statement on the nature of Faith and the "Pentad of operative Christianity" prefixed to the work, and Coleridge's Confession of Faith in the first letter,—he will not fail to acknowledge that whatever coincidences, or seeming plagiarisms, there may be, in respect to the relation of the Scriptures to Christianity, yet that the work of Coleridge, independently of his other writings, bears indubitable evidence of its being an integral part of a digested scheme of Christian philosophy and theology, and that the writings of Lessing, though undoubtedly possessing merits of a high character, are fragmentary, critical, controversial, and tentative.

In order, however, to put the reader, unacquainted with the history of German literature, in possession of the data, which may enable him to form a correct judgment on the point at issue, it may be necessary to explain—and the account is not without its own instructive interest —that Gotthold Ephraim Lessing, one of the most distinguished writers which Germany has produced, mainly contributed by his critical sagacity, his forcible reasoning, and by his lucid, pointed, and nervous style, to awaken a new spirit in almost every branch of literature. It was in 1774, that, feeling the rigidity on the one hand, and the laxity on the other, and the utter shallowness on all sides, of the prevailing theology, he began to publish, in his *Beiträge zur Geschichte und Littera-tur aus den Schätzen der Herzoglichen Bibliothek zu Wolfenbüttel,* the notorious essays, commonly called the Wolfenbüttel Fragments, now known to have been the work of the elder Reimarus, but which were long attributed to Lessing himself. These papers contain a bitter and factious attack on all revealed religion, though it cannot be denied that they proceed from a man, who was nevertheless sincere and earnest in the search for truth. At the conclusion of these fragments, which are five in number, and in addition to remarks appended to each, Lessing expresses himself to the following effect:—

"And now enough of these Fragments!—He, among my readers, who would rather have had me spare them altogether, is assuredly more timid than well-informed. He may be a very devout Christian, but a very enlightened one he certainly is not. He may be a sincere well-wisher to his religion, but he ought also to have more confidence in it.

"For in how many ways may not these objections and difficulties be met! And suppose that absolutely no answer can be given?—What then? The learned theologian might indeed be at length embarrassed: but the Christian likewise! He certainly not. To the former it might be a source of perplexity to see the props, which he designed for the support of religion thus shaken; to find the buttresses thrown down, by which, God willing, he would have secured it. But how do this man's hypotheses and explanations and proofs concern the Christian? For him it is already a fact—that Christianity, which he feels to be so true, in which he feels so blessed.—When the paralytic patient feels the beneficial shocks of the electric spark, what does he care whether Nollett or Franklin, or whether neither the one nor the other, is right?—

"In short, the Letter is not the Spirit and the Bible is not Religion. Consequently objections to the letter and the Bible are not objections to the Spirit and Religion.

"For the Bible manifestly contains more than belongs essentially to Religion, and it is a mere hypothesis that the Bible must be equally infallible in that which is superadded. Besides the Religion was there before a Bible existed. Christianity existed before Evangelists and Apostles had written. There elapsed a long period before the first of them wrote, and a very considerable one before the whole Canon was completed. Much, therefore, as may depend upon these writings, yet it is impossible that the whole truth of the Religion can rest upon them. If there was a period, in which the Christian religion was already thus spread, in which it had already possessed itself of so many souls, and in which as yet not a letter of that which has come down to us had been penned, then it is possible also that all, which Evangelists and Apostles have written, might have been lost, and yet that the religion taught by them might have remained. The Christian religion is not true because the Evangelists and Apostles taught it, but they taught it because it is true. Written traditions must be interpreted by their internal truth, and all the written traditions can give Religion no internal truth, if it have none.

"This, then, would be the general answer to a large portion of these Fragments—as before said, in the worst case."—Lessing's *Schriften*, vol. v, pp. 17–20.

It is principally in this remarkable passage, and in the papers, which arose out of them in the celebrated controversy with the Haupt Pastor Göze of Hamburg, that the reader will find the evidence that he stands in need of for arriving at a satisfactory solution of the question, which is here submitted to his decision: and in order to facilitate the comparison, which he may be expected to institute, the passages in Lessing, and those in the "Confessions," which either in thought or language may be supposed to have been derived from them, have been brought under review in the following paragraphs.

Thus it will be seen that one of Lessing's main propositions is the essential difference between Religion, that is the Christian, as inward and spiritual truth and as an historical fact. He says: "The Letter is not the Spirit, and the Bible is not Religion;" and he adds: "Written traditions must be interpreted by their internal truth, and all the written traditions can give Religion no internal truth, if it have none." The meaning of Lessing appears to be that Religion implies the inward evidence of spiritual truths, which the history of their revelation cannot supply.

In thus requiring an internal evidence for Christianity, we are reminded of the position in the "Confessions," at p. 64, in Letter IV: "The truth revealed through Christ has its evidence in itself, and the proof of its divine authority in its fitness to our nature and needs." Now it may be admitted that Coleridge herein adopts a similar view to that expressed by Lessing, derived from the principle, common to both, that the evidence, which is the chief and primary in importance, for the truths of Christianity, is not to be sought in the historical documents connected with their revelation, but is of an internal character. But it will not be denied that Lessing has nowhere clearly explained what he means by the internal truth (*innere Wahrheit*) which he requires for the interpretation of the written traditions, and that the attempts, which he made to solve philosophically the problems of religion are imperfect and unsatisfactory. He saw indeed that the faith of a Christian, as the vital principle of his spiritual life, is a somewhat very different to the belief, which consists in the mere assent of the understanding to the facts narrated in the Scriptures, even when these facts are the records of the publications of truths, and, as we have seen above, he hesitated not to say that Christianity might have been operative had the Scriptures been lost:—he, in short, maintains that the Scriptures are not essentially the Christian religion itself, but simply the history of its foundation. But though he distinguishes the letter and the spirit, he nowhere tells us what the letter and what the spirit respectively are, and we are left in doubt as to what the Bible contains, and what the Christian religion truly is.

On the other hand, if Coleridge was indebted to his predecessor, it was not assuredly for inforcing the necessity of internal evidence so understood as implying that religion requires the conviction and devotion of the individual, his fealty, head and heart, to the truth in Christ; for this, it may be presumed, is the principle avowed by every sincere believer in the truth of Christianity. Neither could Lessing have first taught him the value of ascertaining the reasonableness of Christianity, independently of its divine institution; for attempts to rationalise the doctrines of Christian faith have been exhibited from the times of the earliest Heathen converts down to the present age, called forth especially by the attacks of infidels. Lessing might indeed have suggested to him the fallacy of considering the Scriptures as the revelation itself and the sole criterion of truth, to which the human reason is to bow as to an infallible oracle forbidding all further questioning, and of mistaking a past fact for an ever-present operative principle and agency. But it is evident that, in claiming for the truth through Christ an "evidence in itself, and the proof of its divine authority in its fitness to our nature and needs," Coleridge appealed to a higher and more comprehensive principle than any to be found in Lessing's writings, namely the influence of the indwelling Reason, "the true Light, which lighteth every man that cometh into the world."[1] It will be seen too, if the reader will take the trouble of perusing attentively the remainder of the letter, from the above quotation taken from p. 64 of the "Confessions," that Coleridge's argument differs from anything which is to be found in Lessing, and that Coleridge, in finding and affirming the truth of Christianity by its fitness to our nature and deeds, derives from this consonance a proof of the authenticity and divine inspiration of the Scriptures. Nor ought it to be forgotten that Coleridge ever

[1] Or, *The light that cometh into the world,—which lighteth every man:* the Word that was made flesh, the sole source of spiritual light to all mankind.

inculcated that Religion must be both Fact and Idea;—that the truths
of Reason, which are implied in Christianity, would constitute only
a system of speculative philosophy, and would cease to be practical,
were they not equally the living principles of the moral world, and
had they not become organic constituents of the history of man and
abiding realities for every man not conscience-proof.

The reader, then, can scarcely doubt that the obligations of Coleridge
to Lessing were slight, if any, in the passage, which we have above
noticed; and probably, if no other connection between the two writers
could have been traced, the comparison would have been deemed
superfluous. But there yet remain certain other parts in the "Confessions" which, in conformity with our design, may not be passed over.

Lessing, it will be seen in the foregoing translation says: "The Christian religion is not true because the Evangelists and Apostles taught it,
but they taught it because it is true." In the VIth Letter of the "Confessions," p. 68, Coleridge asks: "Is it safer for the individual and more
conducive to the interests of the Church of Christ, in its twofold character of pastoral and militant, to conclude thus:—The Bible is the Word
of God, and therefore true, holy, and in all parts unquestionable;—
or thus,—The Bible, considered in reference to its declared ends and
purposes, is true and holy, and for all who seek truth with humble
spirits an unquestionable guide and therefore it is the Word of God?"
—He then proceeds to show that the latter is the safer conclusion.

Now, though it be at once admitted, that the propositions of the
two writers are different, yet on reflection it will be found that they
have this thought in common: Christian teaching does not derive its
truth from authority, but derives its authority from its truth. The passage in Lessing may have suggested, therefore, that in the "Confessions:" but it is equally clear that it contains only a renewal of the
same argument, which we have discussed in the preceding paragraphs
on the primary importance of ascertaining the eternal truths on which
Christianity is founded, in preference to resting its truth on historical
evidence; and if the reader has been convinced that Coleridge's
principle had a deeper source than appears, or is implied, in Lessing's
theological essays, it can matter little, if at all, whether the passage
quoted from Lessing suggested the query and its answer, which we
find in the "Confessions."

But in a note on the opposite opinions, which the query involves,

(namely, The Bible is true and holy, because it is the word of God;
or the Bible is the word of God because it is true and holy)—Coleridge
says: "It is remarkable that both parties might appeal to the same text
of St. Paul,—πᾶσα γραφὴ θεόπνευστος καὶ ὠφέλιμος πρὸς διδασκαλίαν, κ. τ. λ. (2 Tim. iii. 16), which favours the one or other
opinion accordingly as the words are construed; and which, again, is
the more probable construction, depends in great measure on the preference given to one or other of two different readings, the one having,
and the other omitting, the conjunction copulative καί."[1] In one of
the controversial tracts, which arose out of the passage translated to
precede these remarks, Lessing says: "And the πᾶσα γραφὴ of Paul!
—Another construction gives the words of Paul so different a meaning; and this construction being just as grammatical, as consonant
with the connection, and having as many ancient and modern biblical
scholars in its favour, as the construction which has been approved of
in the commonest Lutheran *Dogmatica,* I do not at all see why the
reading adopted in the latter should be unconditionally retained. Luther
himself in his translation has preferred the former: he did not read καὶ;
and evil enough, if by a various reading, consisting in the insertion or
omission of a καὶ, the capital passage on the *principium cognoscendi* of
the whole of theology, is rendered so extremely equivocal."—Lessing's
Schriften, vol. vi, p. 92.

Again, in Lessing's observations on the Wolfenbüttel Fragments,
the following passage will be found: "For the Bible manifestly contains more than belongs essentially to religion, and it is a mere hypothesis that the Bible must be equally infallible in that which is superadded." On turning to the "Confessions," Letter IV, p. 61, we find:
—"I, who hold that the Bible contains the religion of Christians, but
who dare not say that whatever is contained in the Bible is the Christian
religion," &c.; and at p. 57 in the same letter: "But let a man be once
fully persuaded that there is no difference between the two positions—
'The Bible contains the Religion revealed by God'—and—'Whatever
is contained in the Bible is religion, and was revealed by God;' and that
whatever can be said of the Bible, collectively taken, may and must be

[1] The English version is: "All scripture is given by inspiration of God, and is
profitable, &c." By adopting the reading with the omission of the conjunction
καὶ it might have been rendered as in some foreign versions of the Bible is the
case: "All scripture, given by inspiration of God, is profitable, &c." See the note
by the late editor, p. 68.

said of each and every sentence of the Bible, taken for and by itself; and I no longer wonder at these paradoxes."

Subsequently in a controversial tract, written in reply to an attack by Pastor Göze on the position: "The Bible manifestly contains more than belongs essentially to Religion,"—Lessing thus expresses himself (*Kl. Schrift.* vol. vi, p. 85):—"I am shocked! I deny that the Bible *contains* Religion? I? Where? In that which immediately goes before? Hardly in saying that the Bible *is* not Religion itself? Or is it in saying this? Is it thus, my dear Pastor, that you treat all your opponents? Do the words 'to be' and 'to contain' mean the same? Are these identical positions: 'The Bible *contains* Religion;' and 'The Bible *is* Religion?'"
—At p. 86, *ibid.,* he thus proceeds: "As if there were not a little in the Bible, which absolutely neither serves the purpose of explanation nor of confirmation even of the most insignificant tenet of religion! What other sound Lutheran Theologians have maintained with regard to whole books of the Bible, I may surely affirm of particular notices in this or that book. At the least a man must be a Rabbi or a Homilist in order to puzzle out a possibility or a play on words, by which the Hajiemim of Ana, the Crethi and Plethi of David, the mantle which Paul forgot at Troas, and a hundred other such things, can be brought into any connection with religion."

The similarity in thought and language to the quotation in the preceding paragraph needs no comment; but the circumstance is rendered more striking by finding in the "Confessions," at p. 56, the following: "But every word and syllable existing in the original text of the Canonical Books from the *Cherethi* and Phelethi of David, &c."—and at p. 80, "*St. Paul's cloak left at Troas.*"

In the controversial tract of Lessing's, from which the quotation above given is translated, the Author immediately afterwards proceeds to say, p. 87, *ibid.*: "Therefore the position—The Bible contains more than essentially belongs to Religion—is without limitation true. It may likewise be infinitely more serviceable to Religion by its due use, than it can be prejudicial by its misuse. Misuse is especially to be apprehended; and I should have no objection to a provision beforehand against it." The mischiefs accruing to Religion from the opposite opinion, namely (to use Coleridge's words) "that the Bible not only contains, but constitutes, the Christian Religion," are forcibly and eloquently urged in the IVth Letter of the "Confessions," especially in the passage, too long for quotation, which begins (p. 58) at the words—"when in my third letter," and terminates (p. 59) with the words—"you will have no difficulty in determining the quality and character of a dogma, which could engraft such fruits on such a tree." But though the substance of this paragraph, and of the ensuing, beginning with the sentence (p. 60)—"The Bible is the appointed conservatory, an indispensable criterion, and continual source and support of true Belief," is a glorious explication of the position advanced by Lessing, yet it will scarcely be doubted that the reasoning is based upon the same principle, and it would be at least difficult to say how far the train of thought had not been suggested by the pregnant words of the German author. Though it might be added that, where a principle has been so unfolded and expanded, as has been achieved in the present instance, the probability of a primal suggestion may be safely admitted without impugning the originality of the author, who has given incontestable proofs of his ability to make the thought-germ essentially his own, and in transplanting it to cause it to fructify by the inherent fertility of his own mind.

Further, it will be recollected that Lessing, in the summary reply to the Wolfenbüttel Fragments, says:—"It is possible also that all which Apostles and Evangelists have written might have been lost, and yet that the religion taught by them might have remained." It appears that this drew upon him not only the attacks of Pastor Göze, but of other theologians, averse to the deference which it appeared to imply to the Romish doctrine of Tradition: and in reply to Doctor Walch, in the *Briefe an verschiedene Gottesgelehrten,* vol. xvii of his Works, p. 124, he says—"Because the Apostles have left writings behind them is it therefore not necessary to take any heed of Tradition? And was this the true meaning of Irenæus? Not at all; and your Reverence should have assuredly allowed his question to stand: *Quid autem, si neque Apostoli quidem Scripturas reliquissent, nonne oportebat ordinem sequi Traditionis?*" He then goes on to show that what Irenæus meant by *Veritatis Traditionem,* or *Veterem Traditionem,* is only the Confession of faith, Creed or baptismal formulary; and after speaking of St. Augustine's *Sermones in Traditione Symboli,* he adds: "And Irenæus, who uses the same words, is it to be supposed that he did not mean the same thing, when in speaking of the faithful among the Barbarian tribes, who could not read the writings of the Apostles, he says—"*sine*

charta et atramento scriptam habent per Spiritum in cordibus suis salutem?"
Or as we read the quotation, also used in the *Kl. Schrift.*, vol. vi, p. 121
—*"Cui assentiunt multæ gentes barbarorum, eorum qui in Christum
credunt, sine charta et atramento scriptam habentes per Spiritum in cordibus
suis salutem."* Now if we turn to the "Confessions" the same quotation
will be found from Irenæus in Letter VI., at p. 73; but though the
additional references show that they were not copied from Lessing, it
will not remove the suspicion of the reader that Coleridge was induced
to consult the authors in consequence of his study of Lessing's writings.
It is true, however, that Coleridge seems to have attached a larger
meaning and higher importance to the *regula fidei* or *sacramentum
symboli* than Lessing did, namely, as "the universals of Christian Faith."
See the "Confessions," p. 73.

It may be also observed that Coleridge differed from Lessing in the
view which the latter took of the use of the writings of the Apostles
by the early Church. In the letter to Dr. Walch, above referred to,
Lessing says: "The words of Irenæus are—*Non enim per alios disposi-
tionem nostræ salutis cognovimus, quam per eos, per quos Evangelium
pervenit ad nos, quod quidem tunc præconaverunt, postea vero per Dei
voluntatem in Scripturis nobis tradiderunt, fundamentum et columnam fidei
nostræ futurum.* Are these words intended to say that the Scriptures have
become the foundation and support of our faith? Certainly not!
Were this the meaning, assuredly *futuris* must have been substituted
for *futurum*; and as the syntax would not have permitted *fundamentum
et columnam futuris*, the alteration must at least have extended to the
substitution of *fundamento* et *columnâ* futuris—that is, if Irenæus
had not chosen a different turn of the period, supposing that he intended
to say what those with Lutheran spectacles pretend so plainly to discern.
Futurum stands in relation to *Evangelium*; and that this, *præconatum,* as
well as *scripturis traditum,* has become the foundation and support of our
faith, is the proper meaning of Irenæus." Upon this passage Coleridge
makes this comment, in a note pencilled on the margin: "Lessing's
logic forsook him here. Surely Irenæus positively asserts that the Christians had no other stable foundation of their faith than the preaching
of the Gospels in the lifetime of the Apostles, and their written Sermons (as we should say, their published Histories and Discourses,)
after their death. But in the age of Irenæus the Apostles were dead:
ergo, the Apostolic writings were then the sole foundation of Christian

knowledge and belief. This clearly contradicts, as far as his opinion weighs, Lessing's assertion that the Christians were to learn it from the Bishops immediately, who again derived its sense from the Holy Ghost. Besides, take *Evangelium* in Lessing's sense, and the passage amounts to this, that we learn that system of faith which the Apostles preached by the system of faith preached by the Apostles; *i.e.,* it amounts to that species of nonsense called a truism, or identical proposition in a duplicate."

In a fly-leaf of the same volume, Coleridge adds: "I cannot discover any weakening of my confutation in the note, in Lessing's after observations. It does not follow that Irenæus and the Catholic Church did not hold the *Evangelium* (= Gospel Doctrine) which the Apostles first preached, and then, in obedience to the Divine Will, committed to writing in order to supply the preaching after their death, *fundamentum et columnam fidei*; because in controversies with Heretics, Irenæus prudently began with proving the regular descent of the dogma from Bishop to Bishop through the Catholic Church; and then proceeded to show the very same doctrine in the Scriptures. Had he begun with the latter, the Heretics might have either quoted another passage seemingly as favourable to their side as Irenæus's to his, or given a different interpretation. But by always giving two arguments, both of undoubted strength, where the Heretics could give only one, he was sure of mastering them. It makes no difference in the sense of the passage whether it be *futur*um or *futur*is;—in the former it would agree with the wine, in the latter with the vessels containing it—*evangelium in scripturis* or *scripturas evangelium nobis tradentes.*

"Lessing appears to me to have mistaken precepts of the Fathers (*plus justo sacerdotalia*) addressed to the mass of Catholic believers (*ideotis*) for declarations concerning the grounds, the existing grounds and pillars of the Faith of the Church itself. Now these were first, the Universal Tradition of the Churches; and second, *Ostensio è Scripturis,* in other words the Scriptures interpreted according to the consonant belief of the Church in all ages. Even such is the doctrine of the Church of England: herein honourably distinguished both from the Roman Catholics, who placed their pretended Traditions and the Power of the existing Church Hierarchs above the Scriptures, and from the Anti-episcopal Protestants, who reject Tradition and Church authority altogether.   "S. T. COLERIDGE."

The only remark which suggests itself in reading the above interesting extracts is, that in aiding the reader to form a correct opinion on Coleridge's theological views, they warn him not to take for granted that the similarity, or coincidence, of his judgment with that of Lessing on certain points leads justly to the conclusion that Coleridge derived or adopted his opinions from Lessing, and still less that he deemed the latter a safe guide on the whole to a sound and satisfactory theology.

Another reminiscence of Lessing is supplied by Coleridge's adoption of the term "Bibliolatry," which will be found at p. 58 of the "Confessions." It seems to have been invented by Lessing, and those, who have any curiosity on the subject, may consider what he himself has to say in vol. xvii, p. 61 of his *Sämmtliche Schriften*, Berlin, 1793.

On the attempts to harmonise Scripture history, our authors again seem to hold nearly the same opinion. Lessing, vol. v, p. 149, says: "I granted the premiss (namely, the discrepancies in the Gospel narrative of the Resurrection urged in the Wolfenbüttel Fragments) because, after manifold sincere attempts not to permit myself to grant it, I convinced myself of the sorry resources of all Gospel Harmonies. For, to speak of them in general, I would confidently undertake, according to the same rules precisely, which they take as their grounds, to bring unconditionally all and every relation of the same event without exception into no less accordance. Where historians agree only in the main point, the method of our Gospel Harmonists bids defiance to all other difficulties. They cannot be imagined so extravagant but that I will have them presently in order; and in each case I will authenticate my procedure with them by the procedure of some celebrated Harmonist."—

Coleridge in the "Confessions," Letter IV, p. 55, says: "For on what other ground can I account for the whimsical *subintelligiturs* of our numerous Harmonists,—for the curiously inferred facts, the inventive circumstantial detail, the complemental and supplemental history, which, in the utter silence of all historians and absence of all historical documents, they bring to light by mere force of logic?"—And in the same paragraph he adds: "Allow me to create chasms *ad libitum*, and *ad libitum* to fill them up with imagined facts and incidents, and I would almost undertake to harmonise Falstaff's account of the rogues in buckram into a coherent and consistent narrative."

The last, and perhaps only other point, which may require notice, is the agreement of these two eminent men on the services of the Scriptures in aid of the intellectual and moral progress of mankind. In Lessing's tract on the Education of the Human Race, Works, vol. v, p. 91, we find the following passage: "They (the Scriptures) for seventeen hundred years have occupied the human understanding more than all other books; have enlightened it more than all other books, even if it be only by means of the light, which the human understanding has itself brought in." In the "Confessions" it is said, p. 69: "For more than a thousand years the Bible, collectively taken, has gone hand in hand with civilisation, science, law,—in short, with the moral and intellectual cultivation of the species, always supporting, and often leading, the way."

The Editor has thus exhibited faithfully, as far as his knowledge extends, the parallel passages which are to be found in the present work and in the theological writings of Lessing, and the reader has therefore the requisite means of forming his own judgment on the obligations, which Coleridge was under to his predecessor. It would be perhaps as idle as it would be dishonest to deny that the agreements of the two authors are more than accidental; and yet it cannot but be apparent that the most striking parallelisms are in passages, which a plagiarist would have avoided as most easily exposing him to detection, and which he might have dispensed with as a worthless portion of the spoil, namely, as merely collateral to, and illustrative of, the main subject. On the other hand, it can scarcely be doubted that in those parts of Coleridge's work, which involve leading principles of vital import to theology and spiritual religion, such as the essential difference between the Letter and the Spirit, and the primary importance of the internal evidence of Christianity—the only proof of his debt to Lessing is the occasional resemblance in language, whilst the principles themselves might have been derived from other sources; though we have every reason to believe they were virtually the offspring of his own mind, and included in the idea, out of which his theology was evolved as a coherent whole. It is indeed highly probable that in developing this scheme and during the process of mental growth, the salient points of the German author, whom he confessedly studied and admired, became so impropriated by, and amalgamated with, his own mind, that they were no longer remembered, or thought of, as outward and alien, and were indeed as little such as the light, the air, and the warmth, which have become incorporated in the growing plant. And if it may be admitted that to Coleridge's mind Lessing's spirit was seminative, excitant, and nutrient, it must also be borne in mind that these, or similar terms, can have no meaning, except as denoting an action upon that which has inward life and energy, and in respect of Coleridge imply the originality, for which every one, acquainted with the individual character of his religious views, would contend.

Let the final judgment of the reader be, however, what it may, he must not forget, in summing up the evidence, that the passages, above collated, with the arguments which they embody form but a small portion of the writings of either author, from which they have been extracted; and no less that they are incidental to works of these authors, which have respectively very different objects. The purpose of Lessing was that of impugning the hostile attempts of an infidel to overthrow the bulwarks of revealed religion, and of defending himself against the attacks of a zealot, who by his intolerant bigotry was injuring the cause which he professed to support: that of Coleridge was the calm investigation of the difference between the right and the superstitious use of the Scriptures.

It entered into the plan of both to determine the true relation of the Scriptures to Christianity, and in this they both agree that the Letter and the Spirit are essentially different, and that whatever importance is otherwise to be attached to the Scriptures, the truth and vital operance of Christianity must depend primarily on its internal evidence. But if it were granted that Lessing was the guide and predecessor of Coleridge in this view, and up to this point, henceforward, whatever may have been the force of the original suggestion, the means of comparison are merged and vanish in the altered and enlarged proportions and in the surpassing growth of Coleridge's work.

He begins by exhibiting the vital and genetic principle, out of which the life of a Christian is to proceed and develop itself. He tells us in the introductory paragraph, p. 1, that Faith is the actuation of the individual Will by the Logos, the living Truth or substantial Reason;— the same of whom St. John says: "In him was life; and the life was the light of men." Thus, according to Coleridge, Faith is the exponent of the inward light or revelation, coextensive with the humanity, which is one and the same with Reason, and is the "principle of the fidelity of man to God, by the subordination of his human will, in all provinces of his nature, to his Reason, as the sum of spiritual Truth, representing and manifesting the Will Divine."

Next in his Confession of Faith, Letter I, p. 40, he sets forth the "Credenda common to all the Fathers of the Reformation," distributed into five classes. In these, that is in the four first, are included the sum of spiritual truth, or the Truths of Reason, which are the downshine of the True Light, τὸ φῶς τὸ ἀληθινὸν ὃ φωτίζει πάντα ἄνθρωπον ἐρχόμενον εἰς τὸν κόσμον. It is not here the fitting place to enter at large upon a subject which requires for its adequate explication and discussion an appropriate investigation and separate work: but in thus stating the essentials of faith or the fundamental principles of Christianity to the Truths of Reason, the reader is warned against confounding the light of divine Reason with "natural reason," or with aught that may be regarded as the exercise of mere human powers of intelligence and more fitly called "human understanding." The source here affirmed is unequivocally divine. How these truths are awakened, developed and perfected, is another, though doubtless important, question. The position of Coleridge, it cannot be doubted, is that the evidence, origination, and acceptance of these truths imply, in order to their spiritual influence, that the will of the individual is enlightened and enlivened thereto by the light and power of one and the same Universal Reason, indwelling in each and every man. As in all other cases the degree of light and power will be in proportion to the capacity of the recipients; and where the light of Reason exists in that degree, which confers on the individual the conscious possession of its powers, it can only be a wilful fault which deprives him of the insight into those eternal verities, which are already inseparably united with his spiritual being.

But, according to the Author of the "Confessions of an Inquiring Spirit," man is not only inwardly gifted, but he is outwardly aided. Revelation has a twofold character:—if on the one hand, Reason is an inward revelation of those eternal truths which are the stuff of the spiritual being of the individual; so, on the other hand, the revelation of God to his creatures is the manifestation of the same Living Truth as the Providence of the world, acting from the beginning of time in the moral development of the human race, and written imperishably in the facts of history. The leading fact of the divine operance in the history of the world is the existence of the Church, the perpetual revelation of the divine Idea working to the restoration of man to his own divine image, and visibly presented in the Community of individuals in whom by divine Grace this idea or power is operative, and more or less effectual;—it is the institution for the development of the Humanity, of that, in every man, which man is intended to be morally and spiritually;—it is the organic living Body, which continually is assimilating to itself all, who are under the conditions of spiritual growth, and of which the invisible spirit and vital principle is the Logos, the divine Humanity, "the Light, the Truth, and the Way."

The documents which attest Revelation, and to the truth of which the divine spirit, even Eternal Living Truth, bears witness, inwardly in every man, are the Scriptures. These exhibit the working of Providence through a succession of ages to the building up of the Christian Church, in the living fact of which, as the final intention contemplated from the beginning, the lineaments and proportions of the various parts of the plan acquire their significance and evidence: and they are for every human being the needful helps, "which are able to make him wise unto salvation."

Being persuaded of nothing more than of this, that whether it be in matter of speculation or of practice, no untruth can possibly avail the patron and defender long, and that things most truly are likewise most behovefully spoken.—*Hooker*.

Any thing will be pretended rather than admit the necessity of internal evidence, or acknowledge, among the external proofs, the convictions and experiences of Believers, though they should be common to all the faithful in every age of the Church. But in all superstition there is a heart of un-belief; and, *vice versa*, where a man's belief is but a super-ficial acquiescence, credulity is the natural result and accom-paniment, if only he be not required to sink into the depths of his being, where the sensual man can no longer draw breath.—*Literary Remains*.

THE PENTAD OF OPERATIVE CHRISTIANITY

Prothesis

Christ, the Word.

Thesis	*Mesothesis,* or the Indifference,	*Antithesis*
The Scriptures.	The Holy Spirit.	The Church.

Synthesis

The Preacher.

The Scriptures, the Spirit, and the Church, are co-ordinate; the indispensable conditions and the working causes of the perpetuity, and continued renascence and spiritual life of Christ still militant. The Eternal Word, Christ from ever-lasting, is the *Prothesis,* or identity;—the Scriptures and the Church are the two poles, or *Thesis* and *Antithesis,* and the Preacher in direct line under the Spirit but likewise the point of junction of the Written Word and the Church, is the *Synthesis.*

This is God's Hand in the World.

LETTERS ON THE INSPIRATION OF THE SCRIPTURES

SEVEN Letters to a friend concerning the bounds between the right, and the superstitious, use and estimation of the Sacred Canon; in which the Writer submissively discloses his own private judgment on the following Questions:—

I. Is it necessary, or expedient, to insist on the belief of the divine origin and authority of all, and every part of the Canonical Books as the condition, or first principle, of Christian Faith?

II. Or, may not the due appreciation of the Scriptures collectively be more safely relied on as the result and consequence of the belief in Christ; the gradual increase—in respect of particular passages—of our spiritual discernment of their truth and authority supplying a test and measure of our own growth and progress as individual believers, without the servile fear that prevents or overclouds the free honour which cometh from love?   I *John* iv. 18.

LETTER I

My dear Friend,

I employed the compelled and most unwelcome leisure of severe indisposition in reading *The Confessions of a fair Saint* in Mr. Carlyle's recent translation of the *Wilhelm Meister,* which might, I think, have been better rendered literally *The Confessions of a Beautiful Soul.*[1] This, acting in conjunction with the concluding sentences of your Letter, threw my thoughts inward on my own religious experience, and gave the immediate occasion to the following Confessions of one, who is neither fair nor saintly, but who—groaning under a deep sense of infirmity and manifold imperfection—feels the want, the necessity, of religious support;—who cannot afford to lose any the smallest buttress, but who not only loves Truth even for itself, and when it reveals itself aloof from all interest, but who loves it with an indescribable awe, which too often withdraws the genial sap of his activity from the columnar trunk, the sheltering leaves, the bright and fragrant flower, and the foodful or medicinal fruitage, to the deep root ramifying in obscurity and labyrinthine way-winning—

> In darkness there to house unknown,
> Far underground,
> Pierc'd by no sound
> Save such as live in Fancy's ear alone,
> That listen for the uptorn mandrake's parting groan!

I should, perhaps, be a happier—at all events a more useful—man if my mind were otherwise constituted. But so it is: and even with regard to Christianity itself, like certain plants, I creep towards the light, even though it draw me away from the more nourishing warmth. Yea, I should do so, even if the light had made its way through a rent in the wall of the Temple. Glad, indeed, and grateful am I, that not in the Temple itself, but only in one or two of the side chapels—not essential to the edifice, and probably not coeval with it—have I found the light absent, and that the rent in the wall has but admitted the free light of the Temple itself.

[1] *Bekenntnisse einer schönen Seele.*—Ed.

I shall best communicate the state of my faith by taking the creed, or system of *credenda,* common to all the Fathers of the Reformation—overlooking, as non-essential, the differences between the several Reformed Churches—according to the five main classes or sections into which the aggregate distributes itself to my apprehension. I have then only to state the effect produced on my mind by each of these, or the *quantum* of recipiency and coincidence in myself relatively thereto, in order to complete my Confession of Faith.

I. The Absolute; the innominable Αὐτοπάτωρ et *Causa Sui,* in whose transcendant I Am, as the Ground, *is* whatever *verily* is:—The Triune God, by whose Word and Spirit, as the transcendant Cause, *exists* whatever *substantially* exists:—God Almighty—Father, Son, and Holy Ghost, undivided, unconfounded, co-eternal. This class I designate by the word, Στάσις.

II. The Eternal Possibilities; the actuality of which hath not its origin in God: *Chaos spirituale:*—'Απόστασις.

III. The Creation and Formation of the heaven and earth by the Redemptive Word:—The Apostasy of Man:—the Redemption of Man:—the Incarnation of the Word in the Son of Man:—the Crucifixion and Resurrection of the Son of Man: the Descent of the Comforter:—Repentance (μετάνοια):—Regeneration:—Faith:—Prayer:—Grace: Communion with the Spirit: Conflict: Self-abasement: Assurance through the righteousness of Christ: Spiritual Growth: Love: Discipline:—Perseverance: Hope in death:—Μετάστασις—'Ανάστασις.

IV. But these offers, gifts, and graces are not for one, or for a few. They are offered to all. Even when the Gospel is preached to a single individual, it is offered to him as to one of a great Household. Not only Man, but, says St. Paul, the whole Creation is included in the consequences of the Fall—τῆς ἀποστάσεως; so also in those of the Change at the Redemption—τῆς μεταστάσεως, καὶ τῆς ἀναστάσεως. We too shall be raised *in the Body.* Christianity is fact no less than truth. It is spiritual, yet so as to be historical; and between these two poles there must likewise be a midpoint, in which the historical and spiritual meet. Christianity must have its history—a history of itself, and likewise the history of its introduction, its spread, and its outward becoming; and, as the midpoint above-mentioned, a portion of these facts must be miraculous, that is, *phænomena* in nature that are beyond nature. Furthermore, the history of all historical nations must in some sense be its history;—in other words, all history must be providential, and this a providence, a preparation, and a looking forward to Christ.

Here, then, we have four out of the five classes. And in all these the sky of my belief is serene, unclouded by a doubt. Would to God that my faith, that faith which works on the whole man, confirming and conforming, were but in just proportion to my belief, to the full acquiescence of my intellect, and the deep consent of my conscience! The very difficulties argue the truth of the whole scheme and system for my understanding, since I see plainly that so must the truth appear, if it be the truth.

V. But there is a Book, of two parts,—each part consisting of several books. The first part—(I speak in the character of an uninterested critic or philologist)—contains the reliques of the literature of the Hebrew people, while the Hebrew was still the living language. The second part comprises the writings, and, with one or two inconsiderable and doubtful exceptions, all the writings of the followers of Christ within the space of ninety years from the date of the Resurrection. I do not myself think that any of these writings were composed as late as A.D. 120; but I wish to preclude all dispute. This Book I resume, as read, and yet unread,—read, and familiar to my mind in all parts, but which is yet to be perused as a whole; or rather, a work, *cujus particulas et sententiolas omnes et singulas recogniturus sum,* but the component integers of which, and their conspiration, I have yet to study. I take up this work with the purpose to read it for the first time as I should read any other work,—as far at least as I can or dare. For I neither can, nor dare, throw off a strong and awful prepossession in its favour—certain as I am that a large part of the light and life, in and by which I see, love, and embrace the truths and the strengths co-organised into a living body of faith and knowledge in the four preceding classes, has been directly, or indirectly derived to me from this sacred volume,—and unable to determine what I do not owe to its influences. But even on this account, and because it has these inalienable claims on my reverence and gratitude, I will not leave it in the power of unbelievers to say that the Bible is for me only what the Koran is for the deaf Turk, and the Vedas for the feeble and acquiescent Hindoo. No; I will retire *up into the mountain,* and hold secret commune with my Bible above the contagious blastments of prejudice, and the fog-blight of selfish superstition. *For fear hath torment.* And what though *my* reason be to the power and splendour of the Scriptures but as the reflected and secondary shine of the moon compared with the solar radiance;—yet the sun endures the occasional co-presence of the unsteady orb, and leaving it visible seems to sanction the comparison. There is a Light higher than all, even *the Word that was in the beginning*;—the Light, of which light itself is but the *shechinah* and cloudy tabernacle; the Word that is light for every man, and life for as many as give heed to it. If between this Word and the written Letter I shall anywhere seem to myself to find a discrepance, I will not conclude that such there actually is; nor on the other hand will I fall under the condemnation of them that would *lie for God*, but seek as I may, be thankful for what I have—and wait.

With such purposes, with such feelings, have I perused the books of the Old and New Testaments,—each book as a whole, and also as an integral part. And need I say that I have met everywhere more or less copious sources of truth, and power, and purifying impulses;— that I have found words for my inmost thoughts, songs for my joy, utterances for my hidden griefs, and pleadings for my shame and my feebleness? In short whatever *finds* me, bears witness for itself that it has proceeded from a Holy Spirit, even from the same Spirit, *which remaining in itself, yet regenerateth all other powers, and in all ages entering into holy souls maketh them friends of God, and prophets.* (Wisd. vii.) And here, perhaps, I might have been content to rest if I had not learned that, as a Christian, I cannot,—must not—stand alone; or if I had not known that more than this was holden and required by the Fathers of the Reformation, and by the Churches collectively, since the Council of Nice at latest; the only exceptions being that doubtful one of the corrupt Romish Church implied, though not avowed, in its equalisation of the Apocryphal Books with those of the Hebrew Canon,[1] and the irrelevant one of the few and obscure Sects who acknowledge no historical Christianity. This somewhat more, in which Jerome, Augustine, Luther, and Hooker, were of one and the same judgment, and less than which not one of them would have tolerated—would it fall within the scope of my present doubts and objections? I hope it would not. Let only their general expressions be interpreted by their

---

[1] *Si quis—(Esdræ primum et secundum, Tobiam, Judith, Esther, &c.)—pro sacris et canonicis non susceperit, . . . anathema sit.* Conc. Trid. Decr. Sess. IV—*Ed.*

treatment of the Scriptures in detail, and I dare confidently trust that it would not. For I can no more reconcile the Doctrine which startles my belief with the practice and particular declarations of these great men, than with the convictions of my own understanding and conscience. At all events—and I cannot too early or too earnestly guard against any misapprehension of my meaning and purpose—let it be distinctly understood that my arguments and objections apply exclusively to the following Doctrine or Dogma. To the opinions which individual divines have advanced in lieu of this doctrine, my only objection, as far as I object, is—that I do not understand them. The precise enunciation of this doctrine I defer to the commencement of the next Letter.

Farewell.

LETTER II

My DEAR FRIEND,

In my last Letter I said that in the Bible there is more that *finds* me than I have experienced in all other books put together; that the words of the Bible find me at greater depths of my being; and that whatever finds me brings with it an irresistible evidence of its having proceeded from the Holy Spirit. But the doctrine in question requires me to believe, that not only what finds me, but that all that exists in the sacred volume, and which I am bound to find therein, was—not alone inspired by, that is, composed by men under the actuating influence of the Holy Spirit, but likewise—dictated by an Infallible Intelligence; —that the writers, each and all, were divinely informed as well as inspired. Now here all evasion, all excuse, is cut off. An Infallible Intelligence extends to all things, physical no less than spiritual. It may convey the truth in any one of the three possible languages,—that of Sense, as objects appear to the beholder on this earth; or that of Science, which supposes the beholder placed in the centre;—or that of Philosophy, which resolves both into a supersensual reality. But whichever be chosen—and it is obvious that the incompatibility exists only between the first and second, both of them being indifferent and of equal value to the third—it must be employed consistently; for an Infallible

Intelligence must intend to be intelligible, and not to deceive. And, moreover, whichever of these three languages be chosen, it must be translatable into Truth. For this is the very essence of the Doctrine, that one and the same intelligence is speaking in the unity of a Person; which unity is no more broken by the diversity of the pipes through which it makes itself audible, than is a tune by the different instruments on which it is played by a consummate musician, equally perfect in all. One instrument may be more capacious than another, but as far as its compass extends, and in what it sounds forth, it will be true to the conception of the master. I can conceive no softenings here which would not nullify the Doctrine, and convert it to a cloud for each man's fancy to shift and shape at will. And this Doctrine, I confess, plants the vineyard of the Word with thorns for me, and places snares in its pathways. These may be delusions of an evil spirit; but ere I so harshly question the seeming angel of light—my reason, I mean, and moral sense in conjunction with my clearest knowledge—I must inquire on what authority this Doctrine rests. And what other authority dares a truly catholic Christian admit as coercive in the final decision, but the declarations of the Book itself,—though I should not, without struggles and a trembling reluctance, gainsay even a universal tradition?

I return to the Book. With a full persuasion of soul respecting all the articles of the Christian Faith, as contained in the first four Classes, I receive willingly also the truth of the history, namely, that the Word of the Lord did come to Samuel, to Isaiah, to others; and that the words which gave utterance to the same are faithfully recorded. But though the origin of the words, even as of the miraculous acts, be supernatural—yet the former once uttered—the latter once having taken their place among the *phænomena* of the senses, the faithful recording of the same does not of itself imply, or seem to require, any supernatural working, other than as all truth and goodness are such. In the books of Moses, and once or twice in the prophecy of Jeremiah, I find it indeed asserted that not only the words were given, but the recording of the same enjoined by the special command of God, and doubtless executed under the special guidance of the Divine Spirit. As to all such passages, therefore, there can be no dispute; and all others in which the words are by the sacred historian declared to have been the Word of the Lord supernaturally communicated, I receive as such with a degree of confidence proportioned to the confidence required of me by the writer himself, and to the claims he himself makes on my belief.

Let us, therefore, remove all such passages, and take each Book by itself; and I repeat that I believe the writer in whatever he himself relates of his own authority, and of its origin. But I cannot find any such claim, as the Doctrine in question supposes, made by these writers, explicitly or by implication. On the contrary, they refer to other documents, and in all points express themselves as sober minded and veracious writers under ordinary circumstances are known to do. But, perhaps, they bear testimony, the successor to his predecessor?—Or some one of the number has left it on record, that by especial inspiration *he* was commanded to declare the plenary inspiration of all the rest?— The passages, which can without violence be appealed to as substantiating the latter position, are so few, and these so incidental,[1]—the conclusion drawn from them involving likewise so obviously a *petitio principii*, namely, the supernatural dictation, word by word, of the book in which the question is found; (for until this is established, the utmost that such a text can prove, is the current belief of the writer's age and country concerning the character of the books, then called the Scriptures;)—that it cannot but seem strange, and assuredly is against all analogy of Gospel Revelation, that such a Doctrine, which, if true, must be an article of faith, and a most important, yea, essential article of faith,—should be left thus faintly, thus obscurely, and, if I may so say, *obitaneously,* declared and enjoined. The time of the formation and closing of the Canon unknown, the selectors and compilers unknown, or recorded by known fabulists: and (more perplexing still,) the belief of the Jewish Church—the belief, I mean, common to the Jews of Palestine and their more cultivated brethren in Alexandria, (no reprehension of which is to be found in the New Testament)— concerning the nature and import of the θεοπνευστία attributed to the precious remains of their Temple Library;—these circumstances are such, especially the last, as in effect to evacuate the Tenet, of which I am speaking, of the only meaning in which it practically means any thing at all, tangible, stedfast, or obligatory. In infallibility there are

[1] With only one seeming exception, the texts in question refer to the Old Testament alone. That exception is 2 *Peter* iii. 16. The word λοιπάς (γραφάς) is, perhaps, not necessarily so to be interpreted; and this very text formed one of the objections to the Apostolic antiquity of the Epistle itself.

no degrees. The power of the High and Holy One is one and the same, whether the sphere, which it fills, be larger or smaller;—the area traversed by a comet, or the oracle of the house, the holy place beneath the wings of the Cherubim;—the Pentateuch of the Legislator, who drew near to the thick darkness where God was, and who spake in the cloud whence the thunderings and lightnings came, and whom God answered by a voice;—or but a Letter of thirteen verses from the affectionate *Elder to the elect lady and her children, whom he loved in the truth*. But at no period was this the judgment of the Jewish Church respecting all the canonical books. To Moses alone—to Moses in the recording no less than in the receiving of the Law—and to all and every part of the five books, called the Books of Moses, the Jewish Doctors of the generation before, and coeval with, the Apostles assigned that unmodified and absolute *theopneusty,* which our divines, in words at least, attribute to the Canon collectively. In fact it was from the Jewish Rabbis,—who, in opposition to the Christian scheme, contended for a perfection in the Revelation by Moses, which neither required nor endured any addition, and who strained their fancies in expressing the transcendancy of the books of Moses in aid of their opinion,—that the founders of the Doctrine borrowed their notions and phrases respecting the Bible throughout. Remove the metaphorical drapery from the doctrine of the Cabbalists, and it will be found to contain the only intelligible and consistent idea of that plenary inspiration, which later divines extend to all the canonical books; as thus:— "The Pentateuch is but *one Word,* even the Word of God; and the letters and articulate sounds, by which this Word is communicated to our human apprehensions, are likewise divinely communicated."

Now, for "Pentateuch" substitute "Old and New Testament," and then I say that this is the doctrine which I reject as superstitious and unscriptural. And yet as long as the conceptions of the Revealing Word and the Inspiring Spirit are identified and confounded, I assert that whatever says less than this, says little more than nothing. For how can absolute infallibility be blended with fallibility? Where is the infallible criterion? How can infallible truth be infallibly conveyed in defective and fallible expressions? The Jewish teachers confined this miraculous character to the Pentateuch. Between the Mosaic and the Prophetic inspiration they asserted such a difference as amounts to a diversity; and between both the one and the other, and the remaining books comprised under the title of *Hagiographa*, the interval was still wider, and the inferiority in kind, and not only in degree, was unequivocally expressed. If we take into account the habit, universal with the Hebrew Doctors, of referring all excellent or extraordinary things to the great First Cause, without mention of the proximate and instrumental causes,—a striking illustration of which may be obtained by comparing the narratives of the same event in the Psalms and in the Historical Books; and if we further reflect that the distinction of the Providential and the Miraculous did not enter into their forms of thinking,—at all events not into their mode of conveying their thoughts,—the language of the Jews respecting the *Hagiographa* will be found to differ little, if at all, from that of religious persons among ourselves, when speaking of an author abounding in gifts, stirred up by the Holy Spirit, writing under the influence of special grace, and the like.

But it forms no part of my present purpose to discuss the point historically, or to speculate on the formation of either Canon. Rather, such inquiries are altogether alien from the great object of my pursuits and studies, which is, to convince myself and others, that the Bible and Christianity are their own sufficient evidence. But it concerns both my character and my peace of mind to satisfy unprejudiced judges, that if my present convictions should in all other respects be found consistent with the faith and feelings of a Christian,—and if in many and those important points they tend to secure that faith and to deepen those feelings—the words of the Apostle,[1] rightly interpreted, do not require their condemnation. Enough, if what has been stated above respecting the general doctrine of the Hebrew Masters, under whom the Apostle was bred, shall remove any misconceptions that might prevent the right interpretation of his words. Farewell.

LETTER III

My dear Friend,

Having in the former two Letters defined the doctrine which I reject, I am now to communicate the views that I would propose to substitute in its place.

[1] 2 Tim. iii. 16.

Before, however, I attempt to lay down on the theological chart the road-place, to which my bark has drifted, and to mark the spot and circumscribe the space, within which I swing at anchor, let me, first, thank you for, and then attempt to answer, the objections,—or at least the questions,—which you have urged upon me.

"The present Bible is the Canon, to which Christ and the Apostles referred?"

Doubtless.

"And in terms which a Christian must tremble to tamper with?"

Yea. The expressions are as direct as strong; and a true believer will neither attempt to divert or dilute their strength.

"The doctrine which is considered as the orthodox view seems the obvious and most natural interpretation of the texts in question?"

Yea, and Nay. To those whose minds are prepossessed by the Doctrine itself,—who from earliest childhood have always meant this doctrine by the very word, Bible,—the doctrine being but its exposition and paraphrase—Yea. In such minds the words of our Lord and the declarations of St. Paul can awaken no other sense. To those on the other hand, who find the doctrine senseless and self-confuting, and who take up the Bible as they do other books, and apply to it the same rules of interpretation,—Nay.

And, lastly, he who, like myself, recognises in neither of the two the state of his own mind,—who cannot rest in the former, and feels, or fears, a presumptuous spirit in the negative dogmatism of the latter,— he has his answer to seek. But so far I dare hazard a reply to the question,—In what other sense can the words be interpreted?—beseeching you, however, to take what I am about to offer but as an attempt to delineate an arc of oscillation,—that the eulogy of St. Paul is in no wise contravened by the opinion, to which I incline, who fully believe the Old Testament collectively, both in the composition and in its preservation, a great and precious gift of Providence;—who find in it all that the Apostle describes, and who more than believe that all which the Apostle spoke of was of divine inspiration, and a blessing intended for as many as are in communion with the Spirit through all ages. And I freely confess that my whole heart would turn away with an angry impatience from the cold and captious mortal, who, the moment I had been pouring out the love and gladness of my soul, while book after book, Law, and Truth, and Example, Oracle and lovely Hymn, and choral Song of ten thousand thousands, and accepted Prayers of Saints and Prophets, sent back, as it were, from Heaven, like doves, to be let loose again with a new freight of spiritual joys and griefs and necessities, were passing across my memory,—at first pause of my voice, and whilst my countenance was still speaking— should ask me, whether I was thinking of the Book of Esther, or meant particularly to include the first six chapters of Daniel, or verses 6—20 of the 109th Psalm, or the last verse of the 137th Psalm? Would any conclusion of this sort be drawn in any other analogous case? In the course of my Lectures on Dramatic Poetry, I, in half a score instances, referred my auditors to the precious volume before me—Shakespeare —and spoke enthusiastically, both in general and with detail of par- ticular beauties, of the plays of Shakespeare, as in all their kinds, and in relation to the purposes of the writer, excellent. Would it have been fair, or according to the common usage and understanding of men, to have inferred an intention on my part to decide the question respecting Titus Andronicus, or the larger portion of the three parts of Henry VI.? Would not every genial mind understand by Shakespeare that unity or total impression comprising, and resulting from, the thousand- fold several and particular emotions of delight, admiration, gratitude excited by his works? But if it be answered, "Aye! but we must not interpret St. Paul as we may and should interpret any other honest and intelligent writer or speaker,"—then, I say, this is the very *petitio principii* of which I complain.

Still less do the words of our Lord[1] apply against my view. Have I not declared—do I not begin by declaring—that whatever is referred by the sacred Penman to a direct communication from God, and where- ever it is recorded that the Subject of the history had asserted himself to have received this or that command, this or that information or assurance, from a superhuman Intelligence, or where the writer in his own person, and in the character of an historian, relates that the *Word of the Lord came* unto priest, prophet, chieftain, or other individual— have I not declared that I receive the same with full belief, and admit its inappellable authority? Who more convinced than I am—who more anxious to impress that conviction on the minds of others—that the Law and the Prophets speak throughout of Christ? That all the inter- mediate applications and realisations of the words are but types and

[1] John v. 39.

4

repetitions—translations, as it were, from the language of letters and articulate sounds into the language of events and symbolical persons?

And here again let me recur to the aid of analogy. Suppose a Life of Sir Thomas More by his son-in-law, or a Life of Lord Bacon by his chaplain; that a part of the records of the Court of Chancery belonging to these periods were lost; that in Roper's or in Rawley's biographical work there were preserved a series of *dicta* and judgments attributed to these illustrious Chancellors, many and important specimens of their table discourses, with large extracts from works written by them, and from some that are no longer extant. Let it be supposed, too, that there are no grounds, internal or external, to doubt either the moral, intellectual, or circumstantial competence of the biographers. Suppose, moreover, that wherever the opportunity existed of collating their documents and quotations with the records and works still preserved, the former were found substantially correct and faithful, the few differences in no wise altering or disturbing the spirit and purpose of the paragraphs in which they were found, and that of what was not collatable, and to which no test *ab extra* could be applied, the far larger part bore witness in itself of the same spirit and origin; and that not only by its characteristic features, but by its surpassing excellence, it rendered the chances of its having had any other author than the giant-mind, to whom the biographer ascribes it, small indeed! Now, from the nature and objects of my pursuits, I have, we will suppose, frequent occasion to refer to one or other of these works; for example, to Rawley's *Dicta et Facta Francisci de Verulam.* At one time I might refer to the work in some such words as,—"Remember what Francis of Verulam said or judged;" or,—"If you believe not me, yet believe Lord Bacon." At another time I might take the running title of the volume, and at another, the name of the biographer;—"Turn to your Rawley! *He* will set you right;" or,—"*There* you will find a depth, which no research will ever exhaust;" or whatever other strong expression my sense of Bacon's greatness and of the intrinsic worth and the value of the proofs and specimens of that greatness, contained and preserved in that volume, would excite and justify. But let my expressions be as vivid and unqualified as the most sanguine temperament ever inspired, would any man of sense conclude from them that I meant—and meant to make others believe—that not only each and all of these anecdotes, adages, decisions, extracts, incidents had been

dictated, word by word, by Lord Bacon; and that all Rawley's own
observations and inferences, all the connectives and disjunctives, all
the recollections of time, place, and circumstance, together with the
order and succession of the narrative, were in like manner dictated
and revised by the spirit of the deceased Chancellor? The answer will
be—must be;—No man in his senses! "No man in his senses—in *this*
instance; but in that of the Bible it is quite otherwise;—for (I take it as
an admitted point that) it—*is* quite otherwise!"

And here I renounce any advantage I might obtain for my argument by restricting the application of our Lord's and the Apostle's
words to the Hebrew Canon. I admit the justice—I have long felt the
full force—of the remark—"We have all that the occasion allowed."
And if the same awful authority does not apply so directly to the
Evangelical and Apostolical writings as to the Hebrew Canon, yet the
analogy of faith justifies the transfer. If the doctrine be less decisively
Scriptural in its application to the New Testament or the Christian
Canon, the temptation to doubt it is likewise less. So at least we are led
to infer; since in point of fact it is the apparent or imagined contrast,
the diversity of spirit which sundry individuals have believed themselves to find in the Old Testament and in the Gospel, that has given
occasion to the doubt;—and, in the heart of thousands who yield a
faith of acquiescence to the contrary, and find rest in their humility,
—supplies fuel to a fearful wish that it were permitted to make a
distinction.

But, lastly, you object, that—even granting that no coercive,
positive reasons for the belief—no direct and not inferred assertions,
—of the plenary inspiration of the Old and New Testament, in the
generally received import of the term, could be adduced, yet, in behalf
of a doctrine so catholic, and during so long a succession of ages
affirmed and acted on by Jew and Christian, Greek, Romish, and
Protestant, you need no other answer than—"Tell me, first, why it
should not be received! Why should I not believe the Scriptures
throughout dictated, in word and thought, by an infallible Intelligence?"—I admit the fairness of the retort; and eagerly and earnestly
do I answer: For every reason that makes me prize and revere these
Scriptures;—prize them, love them, revere them, beyond all other
books! *Why* should I not? Because the Doctrine in question petrifies
at once the whole body of Holy Writ with all its harmonies and

symmetrical gradations,—the flexile and the rigid,—the supporting hard and the clothing soft,—the blood *which is the life*,—the intelligencing nerves, and the rudely woven, but soft and springy, cellular substance, in which all are embedded and lightly bound together. This breathing organism, this glorious *panharmonicon*, which I had seen stand on its feet as a man, and with a man's voice given to it, the Doctrine in question turns at once into a colossal Memnon's head, a hollow passage for a voice, a voice that mocks the voices of many men, and speaks in their names, and yet is but one voice and the same;—and no man uttered it, and never in a human heart was it conceived. *Why* should I not?—Because the Doctrine evacuates of all sense and efficacy the sure and constant tradition, that all the several books bound up together in our precious family Bibles were composed in different and widely distant ages, under the greatest diversity of circumstances, and degrees of light and information, and yet that the composers, whether as uttering or as recording what was uttered and what was done, were all actuated by a pure and holy Spirit, one and the same—(for is there any spirit pure and holy, and yet not proceeding from God—and yet not proceeding in and with the Holy Spirit?)—one Spirit, working diversly,[1] now awakening strength, and now glorifying itself in weakness, now giving power and direction to knowledge, and now taking away the sting from error! Ere the summer and the months of ripening had arrived for the heart of the race; while the whole sap of the tree was crude, and each and every fruit lived in the harsh and bitter principle; even then his Spirit withdrew its chosen ministers from the false and guilt-making centre of Self. It converted the wrath into a form and an organ of love, and on the passing storm-cloud impressed the fair rainbow of promise to all generations. Put the lust of Self in the forked lightning, and would it not be a Spirit of Moloch? But God maketh the lightnings his ministers, fire and hail, vapours and stormy winds fulfilling his word.

Curse ye Meroz, said the angel of the Lord; curse ye bitterly the inhabitants thereof—sang Deborah. Was it that she called to mind any personal wrongs—rapine or insult—that she or the house of Lapidoth had re-

---

[1] I use the adverb *diversly* from the adjective *divers* in order to distinguish the Scriptural and Pauline sense of the word—the sense in which I here use it—from the logical usage of the term *diversely*, from *diverse*, that is, different in kind, heterogeneous. The same Spirit may act and impel diversly, but, being a good Spirit, it cannot act diversely.

ceived from Jabin or Sisera? No; she had dwelt under her palm tree in the depth of the mountain. But she was a *mother in Israel*; and with a mother's heart, and with the vehemency of a mother's and a patriot's love, she had shot the light of love from her eyes, and poured the blessings of love from her lips, on the people that had *jeoparded their lives unto the death* against the oppressors; and the bitterness, awakened and borne aloft by the same love, she precipitated in curses on the selfish and coward recreants who *came not to the help of the Lord, to the help of the Lord, against the mighty*. As long as I have the image of Deborah before my eyes, and while I throw myself back into the age, country, circumstances, of this Hebrew Bonduca in the not yet tamed chaos of the spiritual creation;—as long as I contemplate the impassioned, high-souled, heroic woman in all the prominence and individuality of will and character,—I feel as if I were among the first ferments of the great affections—the proplastic waves of the microcosmic chaos, swelling up against—and yet towards—the outspread wings of the Dove that lies brooding on the troubled waters. So long all is well,— all replete with instruction and example. In the fierce and inordinate I am made to know and be grateful for the clearer and purer radiance which shines on a Christian's paths, neither blunted by the preparatory veil, nor crimsoned in its struggle through the all-enwrapping mist of the world's ignorance: whilst in the self-oblivion of these heroes of the Old Testament, their elevation above all low and individual interests,—above all, in the entire and vehement devotion of their total being to the service of their divine Master, I find a lesson of humility, a ground of humiliation, and a shaming, yet rousing, example of faith and fealty. But let me once be persuaded that all these heart-awakening utterances of human hearts—of men of like faculties and passions with myself, mourning, rejoicing, suffering, triumphing—are but as a *Divina Commedia* of a superhuman—Oh bear with me, if I say— Ventriloquist;—that the royal Harper, to whom I have so often sub- mitted myself as a *many-stringed instrument* for his fire-tipt fingers to traverse, while every several nerve of emotion, passion, thought, that thrids the flesh-and-blood of our common humanity, responded to the touch,—that this *sweet Psalmist of Israel* was himself as mere an instru- ment as his harp, an *automaton* poet, mourner, and supplicant;—all is gone,—all sympathy, at least, and all example. I listen in awe and fear, but likewise in perplexity and confusion of spirit.

Yet one other instance, and let this be the crucial test of the Doctrine. Say that the Book of Job throughout was dictated by an infallible Intelligence. Then re-peruse the book, and still, as you proceed, try to apply the tenet: try if you can even attach any sense or semblance of meaning to the speeches which you are reading. What! were the hollow truisms, the unsufficing half-truths, the false assumptions and malignant insinuations of the supercilious bigots, who corruptly defended the truth:—were the impressive facts, the piercing outcries, the pathetic appeals, and the close and powerful reasoning with which the poor sufferer—smarting at once from his wounds, and from the oil of vitriol which the orthodox *liars of God* were dropping into them —impatiently, but uprightly and holily, controverted this truth, while in will and in spirit he clung to it;—were both dictated by an infallible Intelligence?—Alas! if I may judge from the manner in which both indiscriminately are recited, quoted, appealed to, preached upon, by the *routiniers* of desk and pulpit, I cannot doubt that they think so,—or rather, without thinking, take for granted that so they are to think;— the more readily, perhaps, because the so thinking supersedes the necessity of all after-thought.

Farewell.

LETTER IV

MY DEAR FRIEND,

You reply to the conclusion of my Letter: "What have we to do with *routiniers? Quid mihi cum homunculis putata putide reputantibus?* Let nothings count for nothing, and the dead bury the dead! Who but such ever understood the Tenet in this sense?"—

In what sense then, I rejoin, do others understand it? If, with exception of the passages already excepted, namely, the recorded words of God—concerning which no Christian can have doubt or scruple,— the Tenet in this sense be inapplicable to the Scripture, destructive of its noblest purposes, and contradictory to its own express declarations,— again and again I ask:—What am I to substitute? What other sense is conceivable that does not destroy the doctrine which it professes to interpret—that does not convert it into its own negative? As if a geometrician should name a sugar loaf an ellipse, adding—"By which term I here mean a cone;"—and then justify the misnomer on the pretext that the ellipse is among the conic sections! And yet—notwithstanding the repugnancy of the Doctrine, in its unqualified sense, to Scripture, Reason, and Common Sense theoretically, while to all practical uses it is intractable, unmalleable, and altogether unprofitable —notwithstanding its irrationality, and in the face of your expostulation, grounded on the palpableness of its irrationality,—I must still avow my belief that, however flittingly and unsteadily, as through a mist, it *is* the Doctrine which the generality of our popular divines receive as orthodox, and this the sense which they attach to the words.

For on what other ground can I account for the whimsical *subintelligiturs* of our numerous harmonists,—for the curiously inferred facts, the inventive circumstantial detail, the complemental and supplemental history which, in the utter silence of all historians and absence of all historical documents, they bring to light by mere force of logic? —And all to do away some half score apparent discrepancies in the chronicles and memoirs of the Old and New Testaments;—discrepancies so analogous to what is found in all other narratives of the same story by several narrators,—so analogous to what is found in all other known and trusted histories by contemporary historians, when they are collated with each other, (nay, not seldom when either historian is compared with himself,) as to form in the eyes of all competent judges a characteristic mark of the genuineness, independency, and (if I may apply the word to a book,) the veraciousness of each several document; a mark the absence of which would warrant a suspicion of collusion, invention, or at best of servile transcription;—discrepancies so trifling in circumstance and import, that, although in some instances it is highly probable, and in all instances, perhaps, possible that they are only apparent and reconcilable, no wise man would care a straw whether they were real or apparent, reconciled or left in harmless and friendly variance. What, I ask, could have induced learned and intelligent divines to adopt or sanction subterfuges, which, neutralising the ordinary *criteria* of full or defective evidence in historical documents, would, taken as a general rule, render all collation and cross-examination of written records ineffective, and obliterate the main character by which authentic histories are distinguished from those traditional tales, which each successive reporter enlarges and fashions to his own fancy and purpose, and every different edition of which more or less contradicts the other? Allow me to create chasms *ad libitum,* and *ad libitum* to fill them up with imagined facts and incidents, and I would almost undertake to harmonise Falstaff's account of the rogues in buckram into a coherent and consistent narrative. What, I say, could have tempted grave and pious men thus to disturb the foundation of the Temple, in order to repair a petty breach or rat-hole in the wall, or fasten a loose stone or two in the outer court, if not an assumed necessity arising out of the peculiar character of Bible history?

The substance of the syllogism, by which their procedure was justified to their own minds, can be no other than this. That, without which two assertions—both of which *must* be alike true and correct— would contradict each other, and consequently be, one or both, false or incorrect, must itself be true. But every word and syllable existing in the original text of the Canonical Books, from the *Cherethi* and *Phelethi*[1] of David to the name in the copy of a family register, the site of a town, or the course of a river, were dictated to the sacred *amanuensis* by an infallible Intelligence. Here there can be neither more nor less. Important or unimportant gives no ground of difference; and the number of the writers as little. The secretaries may have been many,— the historian was one and the same, and he infallible. This is the *minor* of the syllogism; and if it could be proved, the conclusion would be at least plausible; and there would be but one objection to the procedure, namely, its uselessness. For if it have been proved already, what need of proving it over again, and by means—the removal, namely, of apparent contradictions—which the infallible Author did not think good to employ? But if it have not been proved, what becomes of the argument which derives its whole force and legitimacy from the assumption.

In fact, it is clear that the harmonists and their admirers held and understood the Doctrine literally. And must not that divine likewise have so understood it, who, in answer to a question concerning the transcendant blessedness of Jael, and the righteousness of the act, in which she inhospitably, treacherously, perfidiously, murdered sleep, the confiding sleep, closed the controversy by observing that he wanted no better morality than that of the Bible, and no other proof of an action's being praiseworthy than that the Bible had declared it worthy

[1] 2 Sam. xx. 23; 1 Chron. xviii. 17.—*Ed.*

to be praised;—an observation, as applied in this instance, so slanderous
to the morality and moral spirit of the Bible as to be inexplicable,
except as a consequence of the Doctrine in dispute?—But let a man be
once fully persuaded that there is no difference between the two
positions—"The Bible contains the religion revealed by God"—and
—"Whatever is contained in the Bible is religion, and was revealed
by God;"—and that whatever can be said of the Bible, collectively
taken, may and must be said of each and every sentence of the Bible,
taken for and by itself;—and I no longer wonder at these paradoxes.
I only object to the inconsistency of those who profess the same belief,
and yet affect to look down with a contemptuous or compassionate
smile on John Wesley for rejecting the Copernican system as incompatible therewith; or who exclaim "Wonderful!" when they hear
that Sir Matthew Hale sent a crazy old woman to the gallows in
honour of the Witch of Endor.[1] In the latter instance it might, I
admit, have been an erroneous (though even at this day the all but
universally received) interpretation of the word, which we have rendered by *witch*;—but I challenge these divines and their adherents to
establish the compatibility of a belief in the modern astronomy and

---

[1] He sent two, nor does it appear that the poor creatures were at all crazy.

Rose Cullender and Amy Duny, widows, of Lowestoff, Suffolk, were tried for
witchcraft, on the 10th of March, 1665, at Bury St. Edmunds. Sir M. Hale
told the jury, "that he would not repeat the evidence unto them, lest by so doing
he should wrong the evidence on the one side or the other. Only this he acquainted
them, that they had two things to inquire after: first, whether or no these children
were bewitched; secondly, whether the prisoners at the bar were guilty of it.

"*That there were such creatures as witches, he made no doubt at all. For, first, the
Scriptures had affirmed so much. Secondly, the wisdom of all nations had provided laws
against such persons, which is an argument of their confidence of such a crime.* And
such hath been the judgment of this kingdom, as appears by that Act of Parlia-
ment, which hath provided punishments proportionable to the quality of the
offence. And desired them strictly to observe their evidence; and desired the
great God of heaven to direct their hearts in the weighty thing they had in hand.
For to condemn the innocent, and to let the guilty go free were both an abomina-
tion to the Lord."

They were found guilty on thirteen indictments. The bewitched got well of all
their pains the moment after the conviction; "only Susan Chandler felt a pain
like pricking of pins in her stomach."

"The Judge and all the Court felt fully satisfied with the verdict, and thereupon
gave judgment against the witches that they should be hanged."

"They were much urged to confess, but would not."

"They were executed on Monday, the 17th of March following, but they
confessed nothing."—*State Trials,* vi, p. 700.—*Ed.*

natural philosophy with their and Wesley's doctrine respecting the
inspired Scriptures, without reducing the doctrine itself to a plaything
of wax;—or rather to a half-inflated bladder, which, when the contents
are rarefied in the heat of rhetorical generalities, swells out round, and
without a crease or wrinkle; but bring it into the cool temperature
of particulars, and you may press, and as it were except, what part
you like—so it be but one part at a time—between your thumb and
finger.

Now I pray you, which is the more honest, nay, which the more
reverential, proceeding,—to play at fast and loose in this way; or to
say at once, "See here in these several writings one and the same Holy
Spirit, now sanctifying a chosen vessel, and fitting it for the reception
of heavenly truths proceeding immediately from the mouth of God,
and elsewhere working in frail and fallible men like ourselves, and like
ourselves instructed by God's word and laws?"—The first Christian
martyr had the form and features of an ordinary man, nor are we taught
to believe that these features were miraculously transfigured into superhuman symmetry; but *he being filled with the Holy Ghost, they that
looked stedfastly on him, saw his face as it had been the face of an angel.*
Even so has it ever been, and so it ever will be, with all who with
humble hearts and a rightly disposed spirit scan the Sacred Volume.
And they who read it with *an evil heart of unbelief,* and an alien spirit—
what boots for them the assertion that every sentence was miraculously
communicated to the nominal author by God himself? Will it not
rather present additional temptations to the unhappy scoffers, and furnish them with a pretext of self-justification?

When, in my third Letter, I first echoed the question, "Why should
I not?" the answers came crowding on my mind. I am well content,
however, to have merely suggested the main points, in proof of the
positive harm which, both historically and spiritually, our religion
sustains from this Doctrine. Of minor importance, yet not to be
overlooked, are the forced and fantastic interpretations, the arbitrary
allegories and mystic expansions of proper names, to which this indis-
criminate Bibliolatry furnished fuel, spark, and wind. A still greater
evil, and less attributable to the visionary humour and weak judgment
of the individual expositors, is the literal rendering of Scripture in passages, which the number and variety of images employed in different
places, to express one and the same verity, plainly mark out for figura-

tive. And, lastly, add to all these the strange—in all other writings unexampled—practice of bringing together into logical dependency detached sentences from books composed at the distance of centuries, nay, sometimes a *millennium,* from each other, under different dispensations, and for different objects. Accommodations of elder Scriptural phrases—that favourite ornament and garnish of Jewish eloquence—incidental allusions to popular notions, traditions, apologues—(for example, the dispute between the Devil and the Archangel Michael about the body of Moses. *Jude* 9),—fancies and anachronisms imported from the synagogue of Alexandria into Palestine by, or together with, the Septuagint Version, and applied as mere *argumenta ad homines*—(for example, the delivery of the Law by the disposition of Angels, *Acts* vii. 53, *Gal.* iii. 19, *Heb.* ii 2)—these, detached from their context, and, contrary to the intention of the sacred writer, first raised into independent *theses,* and then brought together to produce or sanction some new *credendum,* for which neither separately could have furnished a pretence! By this strange mosaic, Scripture texts have been worked up into passable likenesses of Purgatory, Popery, the Inquisition, and other monstrous abuses. But would you have a Protestant instance of the superstitious use of Scripture arising out of this dogma? Passing by the Cabala of the Hutchinsonian School as the dotage of a few weak-minded individuals, I refer you to Bishop Hacket's Sermons on the Incarnation. And if you have read the same author's Life of Archbishop Williams, and have seen and felt (as every reader of this latter work must see and feel,) his talent, learning, acuteness, and robust good sense, you will have no difficulty in determining the quality and character of a dogma, which could engraft such fruits on such a tree.'[1]

It will perhaps appear a paradox, if, after all these reasons, I should

---

[1] "Did not the life of Archbishop Williams prove otherwise, I should have inferred from these Sermons that Hacket from his first boyhood had been used to make themes, epigrams, copies of verses, and the like on all the feasts and festivals of the Church; had found abundant nourishment for this humour of points, quirks, and quiddities, in the study of the Fathers and glossers; and remained a *junior soph* all his life long." . . . "Let any competent judge read Hacket's Life of Archbishop Williams, and then these Sermons, and so measure the stultifying, nugifying, effect of a blind and uncritical study of the Fathers, and the exclusive prepossession in favour of their authority in the minds of many of our Church dignitaries in the reign of Charles I."—*Lit. Remains,* III, pp. 175 and 183.—*Ed.*

avow that they weigh less in my mind against the Doctrine, than the motives usually assigned for maintaining and enjoining it. Such, for instance, are the arguments drawn from the anticipated loss and damage that would result from its abandonment; as that it would deprive the Christian world of its only infallible arbiter in questions of Faith and Duty, suppress the only common and inappellable tribunal; that the Bible is the only religious bond of union and ground of unity among Protestants, and the like. For the confutation of this whole reasoning it might be sufficient to ask:—Has it produced these effects? Would not the contrary statement be nearer to the fact? What did the Churches of the first four centuries hold on this point? To what did they attribute the rise and multiplication of heresies? Can any learned and candid Protestant affirm that there existed and exists no ground for the charges of Bosuet and other eminent Romish divines? It is no easy matter to know how to handle a party maxim, so framed that, with the exception of a single word, it expresses an important truth, but which by means of that word is made to convey a most dangerous error.

The Bible is the appointed conservatory, an indispensable criterion, and a continual source and support of true Belief. But that the Bible is the sole source; that it not only contains, but constitutes, the Christian Religion; that it is, in short, a Creed, consisting wholly of articles of Faith; that consequently we need no rule, help, or guide, spiritual or historical, to teach us what parts are and what are not articles of Faith —all being such—and the difference between the Bible and the Creed being this, that the clauses of the latter are all unconditionally necessary to salvation, but those of the former conditionally so, that is, as soon as the words are known to exist in any one of the canonical Books; and that, under this limitation, the belief is of the same necessity in both, and not at all affected by the greater or lesser importance of the matter to be believed;—this scheme differs widely from the preceding, though its adherents often make use of the same words in expressing their belief. And this latter scheme, I assert, was brought into currency by and in favour of those by whom the operation of grace, the aids of the Spirit, the necessity of regeneration, the corruption of our nature, in short, all the peculiar and spiritual mysteries of the Gospel were explained and diluted away.

And how have these men treated this very Bible?—I, who indeed prize and reverence this sacred library, as of all outward means and conservatives of Christian faith and practice the surest and the most reflective of the inward Word;—I, who hold that the Bible contains the religion of Christians, but who dare not say that whatever is contained in the Bible is the Christian religion, and who shrink from all question respecting the comparative worth and efficacy of the written Word as weighed against the preaching of the Gospel, the discipline of the Churches, the continued succession of the Ministry, and the communion of Saints, lest by comparing I should seem to detach them; —I tremble at the processes, which the Grotian divines without scruple carry on in their treatment of the sacred Writers, as soon as any texts declaring the peculiar tenets of our Faith are cited against them,— even tenets and mysteries which the believer at his baptism receives as the title-writ and bosom-roll of his adoption; and which, according to my scheme, every Christian born in Church-membership ought to bring with him to the study of the sacred Scriptures as the master-key of interpretation. Whatever the doctrine of infallible dictation may be in itself, in *their* hands it is to the last degree nugatory, and to be paralleled only by the Romish tenet of Infallibility,—in the existence of which all agree, but where, and in whom, it exists is still matter of debate. Every sentence found in a canonical Book, rightly interpreted, contains the *dictum* of an infallible Mind;—but what the right interpretation is,—or whether the very words now extant are corrupt or genuine—must be determined by the industry and understanding of fallible, and alas! more or less prejudiced theologians.

And yet I am told that this Doctrine must not be resisted or called in question, because of its fitness to preserve unity of faith, and for the prevention of schism and sectarian by-ways!—Let the man who holds this language trace the history of Protestantism, and the growth of sectarian divisions, ending with Dr. Hawker's *ultra*-Calvinistic Tracts, and Mr. Belsham's New Version of the Testament. And then let him tell me that for the prevention of an evil which already exists, and which the boasted preventive itself might rather seem to have occasioned, I must submit to be silenced by the first learned Infidel, who throws in my face the blessing of Deborah, or the cursings of David, or the Grecisms and heavier difficulties in the biographical chapters of the Book of Daniel, or the hydrography and natural philosophy of the Patriarchal ages.—I must forego the means of silencing, and the prospect of convincing, an alienated brother, because I must not thus answer:—"My Brother! What has all this to do with the truth and the worth of Christianity? If you reject *à priori* all communion with the Holy Spirit, there is indeed a chasm between us, over which we cannot even make our voices intelligible to each other. But if—though but with the faith of a Seneca or an Antonine—you admit the co-operation of a divine Spirit in souls desirous of good, even as the breath of heaven works variously in each several plant according to its kind, character, period of growth, and circumstance of soil, clime, and aspect;—on what ground can you assume that its presence is incompatible with all imperfection in the subject—even with such imperfection as is the natural accompaniment of the unripe season? If you call your gardener or husbandman to account for the plants or crops he is raising, would you not regard the social purpose in each, and judge of each by that which it was tending to? Thorns are not flowers, nor is the husk serviceable. But it was not for its thorns, but for its sweet and medicinal flowers that the rose was cultivated; and he who cannot separate the husk from the grain, wants the power because sloth or malice has prevented the will. I demand for the Bible only the justice which you grant to other books of grave authority, and to other proved and acknowledged benefactors of mankind. Will you deny a spirit of wisdom in Lord Bacon, because in particular facts he did not possess perfect science, or an entire immunity from the positive errors which result from imperfect insight? A Davy will not so judge his great predecessor. For he recognises the spirit that is now working in himself, and which under similar defects of light and obstacles of error had been his guide and guardian in the morning twilight of his own genius. Must not the kindly warmth awaken and vivify the seed, in order that the stem may spring up and rejoice in the light? As the genial warmth to the informing light, even so is the pre-disposing Spirit to the revealing Word."

If I should reason thus—but why do I say *if*?—I have reasoned thus with more than one serious and well-disposed Sceptic; and what was the answer?—"*You* speak rationally, but seem to forget the subject. I have frequently attended meetings of the British and Foreign Bible Society, where I have heard speakers of every denomination, Calvinist and Arminian, Quaker and Methodist, Dissenting Ministers and Clergymen, nay, dignitaries of the Established Church,—and still have I heard the same doctrine,—that the Bible was not to be regarded or reasoned about in the way that other good books are or may be;—that the Bible was different in kind, and stood by itself. By some indeed this doctrine was rather implied than expressed, but yet evidently implied. But by far the greater number of the speakers it was asserted in the strongest and most unqualified words that language could supply. What is more, their principal arguments were grounded on the position, that the Bible throughout was dictated by Omniscience, and therefore in all its parts infallibly true and obligatory, and that the men, whose names are prefixed to the several books or chapters, were in fact but as different pens in the hand of one and the same Writer, and the words the words of God himself;—and that on this account all notes and comments were superfluous, nay, presumptuous,—a profane mixing of human with divine, the notions of fallible creatures, with the oracles of Infallibility,—as if God's meaning could be so clearly or fitly expressed in man's as in God's own words! But how often you yourself must have heard the same language from the pulpit!"—

What could I reply to this?—I could neither deny the fact, nor evade the conclusion,—namely, that such is at present the popular belief. Yes—I at length rejoined—I have heard this language from the pulpit, and more than once from men who in any other place would explain it away into something so very different from the literal sense of their words as closely to resemble the contrary. And this, indeed, is the peculiar character of the doctrine, that you cannot diminish or qualify but you reverse it. I have heard this language from men, who knew as well as myself that the best and most orthodox divines have in effect disclaimed the doctrine, inasmuch as they confess it cannot be extended to the words of the sacred Writers, or the particular import,—that therefore the Doctrine does not mean all that the usual wording of it expresses, though what it does mean, and why they continue to sanction this hyperbolical wording, I have sought to learn from them in vain. But let a thousand orators blazon it at public meetings, and let as many pulpits echo it, surely it behoves you to inquire whether you cannot be a Christian on your own faith; and it cannot but be beneath a wise man to be an Infidel on the score of what other men think fit to include in their Christianity!

Now suppose—and, believe me, the supposition will vary little from the fact—that in consequence of these views the Sceptic's mind had gradually opened to the reception of all the truths enumerated in my first Letter. Suppose that the Scriptures themselves from this time had continued to rise in his esteem and affection—the better understood, the more dear; as in the countenance of one, whom through a cloud of prejudices we have at least learned to love and value above all others, new beauties dawn on us from day to day, till at length we wonder how we could at any time have thought it other than most beautiful. Studying the sacred volume in the light and in the freedom of a faith already secured, at every fresh meeting my Sceptic friend has to tell me of some new passage, formerly viewed by him as a dry stick on a rotten branch, which has *budded* and, like the rod of Aaron, *brought forth buds and bloomed blossoms, and yielded almonds.* Let these results, I say, be supposed,—and shall I still be told that my friend is nevertheless an alien in the household of Faith? Scrupulously orthodox as I know you to be, will you tell me that I ought to have left this Sceptic as I found him, rather than attempt his conversion by such means; or that I was deceiving him, when I said to him:—

"Friend! The truth revealed through Christ has its evidence in itself, and the proof of its divine authority in its fitness to our nature and needs;—the clearness and cogency of this proof being proportionate to the degree of self-knowledge in each individual hearer. Christianity has likewise its historical evidences, and these as strong as is compatible with the nature of history, and with the aims and objects of a religious dispensation. And to all these Christianity itself, as an existing Power in the world, and Christendom as an existing Fact, with the no less evident fact of a progressive expansion, give a force of moral demonstration that almost supersedes particular testimony. These proofs and evidences would remain unshaken, even though the sum of our religion were to be drawn from the theologians of each successive century, on the principle of receiving that only as divine, which should be found in all,—*quod semper, quod ubique, quod ab omnibus.* Be only, my Friend! as orthodox a believer as you would have abundant reason to be, though from some accident of birth, country, or education the precious boon of the Bible, with its additional evidence, had up to this moment been concealed from you;—and then read its contents with only the same piety which you freely accord on other occasions to the writings of men, considered the best and wisest of their several ages! What you find therein coincident with your preestablished convictions, you will of course recognise as the revealed Word, while, as you read the recorded workings of the Word and the Spirit in the minds, lives, and hearts of spiritual men, the influence of the same Spirit on your own being, and the conflicts of grace and infirmity in your own soul, will enable you to discern and to know in and by what spirit they spake and acted,—as far at least as shall be needful for you, and in the times of your need.

"Thenceforward, therefore, your doubts will be confined to such parts or passages of the received Canon, as seem to you irreconcilable with known truths, and at variance with the tests given in the Scriptures themselves, and as shall continue so to appear after you have examined each in reference to the circumstances of the Writer or Speaker, the dispensation under which he lived, the purpose of the particular passage, and the intent and object of the Scriptures at large. Respecting these, decide for yourself: and fear not for the result. I venture to tell it you before hand. The result will be, a confidence in the judgment and fidelity of the compilers of the Canon increased by the apparent exceptions. For they will be found neither more nor greater than may well be supposed requisite, on the one hand, to prevent us from sinking into a habit of slothful, undiscriminating, acquiescence, and on the other to provide a check against those presumptuous fanatics, who would rend the *Urim and Thummim from the breastplate of judgment,* and frame oracles by private divination from each letter of each disjointed gem, uninterpreted by the Priest, and deserted by the Spirit, which shines in the parts only as it pervades and irradiates the whole."

Such is the language in which I have addressed a halting friend,— halting, yet with his face towards the right path. If I have erred, enable me to see my error. Correct me, or confirm me.

Farewell.

LETTER V

Yes! my dear Friend, it is my conviction that in all ordinary cases the knowledge and belief of the Christian Religion should precede the study of the Hebrew Canon. Indeed, with regard to both

5

Testaments, I consider oral and catechismal instruction as the preparative provided by Christ himself in the establishment of a visible Church. And to make the Bible, apart from the truths, doctrines, and spiritual experiences contained therein, the subject of a special article of faith, I hold an unnecessary and useless abstraction, which in too many instances has the effect of substituting a barren acquiescence in the letter for the lively *faith that cometh by hearing*; even as the hearing is productive of this faith, because it is the word of God that is heard and preached. (*Rom.* x. 8, 17). And here I mean the written word preserved in the armoury of the Church to be the sword of faith *out of the mouth* of the preacher, as Christ's ambassador and representative (*Rev.* I. 16), and out of the heart of the believer, from generation to generation. Who shall dare dissolve or loosen this holy bond, this divine reciprocality, of Faith and Scripture? Who shall dare enjoin aught else as an object of saving faith, beside the truths that appertain to salvation? The imposers take on themselves a heavy responsibility, however defensible the opinion itself, as an opinion, may be. For by imposing it, they counteract their own purposes. They ante-date questions, and thus in all cases aggravate the difficulty of answering them satisfactorily. And not seldom they create difficulties that might never have occurred. But, worst of all, they convert things trifling or indifferent into mischievous pretexts for the wanton, fearful difficulties for the weak, and formidable objections for the inquiring. For what man *fearing* God dares think any the least point indifferent, which he is required to receive as God's own immediate word miraculously infused, miraculously recorded, and by a succession of miracles preserved unblended and without change?—Through all the pages of a large and multifold volume, at each successive period, at every sentence, must the question recur:—"Dare I believe—do I in my heart believe—these words to have been dictated by an infallible reason, and the immediate utterance of Almighty God?"—No! It is due to Christian charity that a question so awful should not be put unnecessarily, and should not be put out of time. The necessity I deny. And out of time the question must be put, if after enumerating the several articles of the Catholic Faith I am bound to add:—"and further you are to believe with equal faith, as having the same immediate and miraculous derivation from God, whatever else you shall hereafter read in any of the sixty-six books collected in the Old and New Testaments."

I would never say this. Yet let me not be misjudged as if I treated the Scriptures as a matter of indifference. I would not say this: but where I saw a desire to believe, and a beginning love of Christ, I would there say:—"There are likewise sacred Writings, which, taken in connection with the institution and perpetuity of a visible Church, all believers revere as the most precious boon of God, next to Christianity itself, and attribute both their communication and preservation to an especial Providence. In them you will find all the revealed truths, which have been set forth and offered to you, clearly and circumstantially recorded; and, in addition to these, examples of obedience and disobedience both in states and individuals, the lives and actions of men eminent under each dispensation, their sentiments, maxims, hymns, and prayers,—their affections, emotions, and conflicts;—in all which you will recognise the influence of the Holy Spirit, with a conviction increasing with the growth of your own faith and spiritual experience."

Farewell.

LETTER VI

My dear Friend,

In my last two Letters I have given the state of the argument, as it would stand between a Christian thinking as I do, and a serious well-disposed Deist. I will now endeavour to state the argument, as between the former and the advocates for the popular belief,—such of them, I mean, as are competent to deliver a dispassionate judgment in the cause. And again, more particularly, I mean the learned and reflecting part of them, who are influenced to the retention of the prevailing dogma by the supposed consequences of a different view, and, especially, by their dread of conceding to all alike, simple and learned, the privilege of picking and choosing the Scriptures that are to be received as binding on their consciences. Between these persons and myself the controversy[1] may be reduced to a single question:—

---

[1] It is remarkable that both parties might appeal to the same text of St. Paul,—πᾶσα γραφὴ θεόπνευστος καὶ ὠφέλιμος πρὸς διδασκαλίαν, κ. τ. λ. (2 Tim. iii. 16), which favours the one or the other opinion accordingly as the words are

Is it safer for the Individual, and more conducive to the interests of the Church of Christ, in its twofold character of pastoral and militant, to conclude thus:—The Bible is the Word of God, and therefore true, holy, and in all parts unquestionable;—or thus,—The Bible, considered in reference to its declared ends and purposes, is true and holy, and for all who seek truth with humble spirits an unquestionable guide, and therefore it is the Word of God?

In every generation, and wherever the light of Revelation has shone, men of all ranks, conditions, and states of mind have found in this Volume a correspondent for every movement toward the Better felt in their own hearts. The needy soul has found supply, the feeble a help, the sorrowful a comfort; yea, be the recipiency the least that can consist with moral life, there is an answering grace ready to enter. The Bible has been found a spiritual World,—spiritual, and yet at the same time outward and common to all. You in one place, I in another, all men somewhere or at some time, meet with an assurance that the hopes and fears, the thoughts and yearnings that proceed from or tend to, a right spirit in us, are not dreams or fleeting singularities, no voices heard in sleep, or spectres which the eye suffers but not perceives. As if on some dark night a pilgrim, suddenly beholding a bright star moving before him, should stop in fear and perplexity. But lo! traveller after traveller passes by him, and each being questioned

construed; and which, again, is the more probable construction, depends in great measure on the preference given to one or other of two different readings, the one having and the other omitting the conjunction copulative καὶ.

[The English version is:—*All Scripture is given by inspiration of God, and is profitable, &c.* And in this rendering of the original the English is countenanced by the established Version of the Dutch Reformed Church:—*Alle de Schrift is van Godt ingegeven, ende is nuttigh, &c.* And by Diodati:—*Tutta la Scrittura è divinamente inspirata, ed util, &c.* And by Martin:—*Toute l'Ecriture est divinement inspirée, et profitable, &c.* And by Beza:—*Tota Scriptura divinitus est inspirata, et utilis, &c.*

The other rendering is supported by the Vulgate:—*Omnis Scriptura, divinitus inspirata, utilis est ad, &c.* By Luther:—*Denn alle Schrift von Gott eingegeben, ist nütze zur, &c.* And by Calmet:—*Toute l'Ecriture, qui est inspirée de Dieu, est utile, &c.* And by the common Spanish translation:—*Toda Escritura, divinamente inspirada, es util para ensñar, &c.* This is also the rendering of the Syriac (Pesch.) and two Arabic Versions, and is followed by Clement of Alexandria, Origen, and most of the Fathers. See the note to Griesbach. Tertullian represents the sense thus:—*Legimus, Omnem Scripturam, œdificationi habilem, divinitus inspirari.* De Habit. Mul. c. iii. Origen has it several times, Θεόπνευστος οὖσα, ὠφέλιμός ἐστι, and once as in the received text.—*Ed.*]

whither he is going, makes answer, "I am following yon guiding Star!" The pilgrim quickens his own steps, and presses onward in confidence. More confident still will he be, if by the way side he should find, here and there, ancient monuments, each with its votive lamp, and on each the name of some former pilgrim, and a record that there he had first seen or begun to follow the benignant Star!

No otherwise is it with the varied contents of the Sacred Volume. The hungry have found food, the thirsty a living spring, the feeble a staff, and the victorious warfarer songs of welcome and strains of music; and as long as each man asks on account of his wants, and asks what he wants, no man will discover aught amiss or deficient in the vast and many-chambered storehouse. But if instead of this, an idler or a scoffer should wander through the rooms, peering and peeping, and either detects, or fancies he has detected here, a rusted sword or pointless shaft, there a tool of rude construction, and superseded by later improvements (and preserved, perhaps, to make us more grateful for them);—which of two things will a sober-minded man,—who from his childhood upward had been fed, clothed, armed, and furnished with the means of instruction from this very magazine,—think the fitter plan?—Will he insist that the rust is not rust, or that it is a rust *sui generis,* intentionally formed on the steel for some mysterious virtue in it, and that the staff and astrolabe of a shepherd-astronomer are identical with, or equivalent to, the quadrant and telescope of Newton or Herschel?—Or will he not rather give the curious inquisitor joy of his mighty discoveries, and the credit of them for his reward?—

Or lastly, put the matter thus. For more than a thousand years the Bible, collectively taken, has gone hand in hand with civilisation, science, law,—in short, with the moral and intellectual cultivation of the species, always supporting, and often leading the way. Its very presence, as a believed Book, has rendered the nations emphatically a chosen race, and this too in exact proportion as it is more or less generally known and studied. Of those nations, which in the highest degree enjoy its influences, it is not too much to affirm, that the differences public and private, physical, moral and intellectual, are only less than what might be expected from a diversity in species. Good and holy men, and the best and wisest of mankind, the kingly spirits of history, enthroned in the hearts of mighty nations, have borne witness to its influences, have declared it to be beyond compare the most perfect instrument, the only adequate organ, of Humanity;—the organ and instrument of all the gifts, powers, and tendencies, by which the individual is privileged to rise above himself—to leave behind, and lose his dividual phantom self, in order to find his true Self in that Distinctness where no division can be,—in the Eternal I Am, the Ever-living Word, of whom all the elect from the arch-angel before the throne to the poor wrestler with the Spirit *until the breaking of day* are but the fainter and still fainter echoes. And are all these testimonies and lights of experience to lose their value and efficiency, because I feel no warrant of history, or Holy Writ, or of my own heart for denying, that in the framework and outward case of this instrument a few parts may be discovered of less costly materials and of meaner workmanship? Is it not a fact that the Books of the New Testament were tried by their consonance with the rule, and according to the analogy, of Faith? Does not the universally admitted canon—that each part of Scripture must be interpreted by the spirit of the whole—lead to the same practical conclusion as that for which I am now contending; —namely, that it is the spirit of the Bible, and not the detached words and sentences, that is infallible and absolute?—Practical, I say, and spiritual too;—and what knowledge not practical or spiritual are we entitled to seek in our Bibles? Is the grace of God so confined,—are the evidences of the present and actuating Spirit so dim and doubtful,— that to be assured of the same we must first take for granted that all the life and co-agency of our humanity is miraculously suspended?

Whatever is spiritual, is *eo nomine* supernatural; but must it be always and of necessity miraculous? Miracles could open the eyes of the body; and he that was born blind beheld his Redeemer. But miracles, even those of the Redeemer himself, could not open the eyes of the self-blinded, of the Sadducean sensualist or the self-rightous Pharisee;— while to have said, *I saw thee under the fig tree,* sufficed to make a Nathanael believe.

To assert and to demand miracles without necessity was the vice of the unbelieving Jews of old; and from the Rabbis and Talmudists the infection has spread. And would I could say that the symptoms of the disease are confined to the Churches of the Apostasy! But all the miracles, which the legends of Monk or Rabbi contain, can scarcely be put in competition, on the score of complication, inexplicableness, the absence of all intelligible use or purpose, and of circuitous self-frustration, with those that must be assumed by the maintainers of this doctrine, in order to give effect to the series of miracles, by which all the nominal composers of the Hebrew nation before the time of Ezra, of whom there are any remains, were successively transformed into *automaton* compositors,—so that the original text should be in sentiment, image, word, syntax, and composition an exact impression of the divine copy! In common consistency the theologians, who impose this belief on their fellow Christians, ought to insist equally on the superhuman origin and authority of the Masora, and to use more respectful terms, than has been their wont of late, in speaking of the false Aristeas's legend concerning the Septuagint. And why the miracle should stop at the Greek Version, and not include the Vulgate, I can discover no ground in reason. Or if it be an objection to the latter, that this belief is actually enjoined by the Papal Church, yet the number of Christians who read the Lutheran, the Genevan, or our own authorised, Bible, and are ignorant of the dead languages, greatly exceeds the number of those who have access to the Septuagint. Why refuse the writ of consecration to these, or to the one at least appointed by the assertors' own Church? I find much more consistency in the opposition made under pretext of this doctrine to the proposals and publications of Kennicot, Mill, Bentley, and Archbishop Newcome.

But I am weary of discussing a tenet, which the generality of divines and the leaders of the Religious Public have ceased to defend, and yet continue to assert or imply. The tendency manifested in this conduct, the spirit of this and the preceding century, on which, not indeed the tenet itself, but the obstinate adherence to it against the clearest light of reason and experience, is grounded,—this it is which, according to my conviction, gives the venom to the error, and justifies the attempt to substitute a juster view. As long as it was the common and effective belief of all the Reformed Churches, (and by none was it more sedulously or more emphatically enjoined than by the great Reformers of our Church,) that by the good Spirit were the spirits tried, and that the light, which beams forth from the written Word, was its own evidence for the children of light;—as long as Christians considered their Bible as a plenteous entertainment, where every guest, duly called and attired, found the food needful and fitting for him, and where each— instead of troubling himself about the covers not within his reach—

beholding all around him glad and satisfied, praised the banquet and thankfully glorified the Master of the feast,—so long did the Tenet —that the Scriptures were written under the special impulse of the Holy Ghost remain safe and profitable. Nay, in the sense, and with the feelings, in which it was asserted, it was a truth—a truth to which every spiritual believer now and in all times will bear witness by virtue of his own experience. And if in the overflow of love and gratitude they confounded the power and presence of the Holy Spirit, working alike in weakness and in strength, in the morning mists and in the clearness of the full day;—if they confounded this communion and coagency of divine grace, attributable to the Scripture generally, with those express, and expressly recorded, communications and messages of the Most High, which form so large and prominent a portion of the same Scriptures;—if, in short, they did not always duly distinguish the inspiration, the imbreathment, of the predisposing and assisting SPIRIT from the revelation of the informing WORD,—it was at worst a harmless hyperbole. It was holden by all, that if the power of the Spirit from without furnished the text, the grace of the same Spirit from within must supply the comment.

In the sacred Volume they saw and reverenced the bounden wheat-sheaf that *stood upright* and had *obeisance* from all the other sheaves— (the writings, I mean, of the Fathers and Doctors of the Church) —sheaves depreciated indeed, more or less, with tares,

> And furrow-weeds,
> Darnel and many an idle flower that grew
> Mid the sustaining corn;

yet sheaves of the same harvest, the sheaves of brethren! Nor did it occur to them, that, in yielding the more full and absolute honour to the sheaf of the highly favoured of their father, they should be supposed to attribute the same worth and quality to the straw-bands which held it together. The bread of life was there. And this in an especial sense was *bread from heaven*; for no where had the same been found wild; no soil or climate dared claim it for its natural growth. In simplicity of heart they received the Bible as the precious gift of God, providential alike in origin, preservation, and distribution, without asking the nice question, whether all and every part were likewise miraculous. The distinction between the providential and the miraculous, between the divine Will working with the agency of natural causes, and the same Will supplying their place by a special *fiat*—this distinction has, I doubt not, many uses in speculative divinity. But its weightiest practical application is shown, when it is employed to free the souls of the unwary and weak in faith from the nets and snares, the insidious queries and captious objections, of the Infidel by calming the flutter of their spirits. They must be quieted, before we can commence the means necessary for their disentanglement. And in no way can this be better effected than when the frightened captives are made to see in how many points the disentangling itself is a work of expedience rather than of necessity;—so easily and at so little loss might the web be cut or brushed away!

First, let their attention be fixed on the history of Christianity as learnt from universal tradition, and the writers of each successive generation. Draw their minds to the fact of the progressive and still continuing fulfilment of the assurance of a few fishermen, that both their own religion, though of divine origin, and the religion of their conquerors, which included or recognised all other religions of the known world, should be superseded by the faith in a man recently and ignominiously executed. Then induce them to meditate on the universals of Christian Faith,—on Christianity, taken as the sum of belief common to Greek and Latin, to Romanist and Protestant. Show them that this and only this is the *ordo traditionis, quam tradiderunt Apostoli iis quibus committebant ecclesias,* and which we should have been bound to follow, says Irenæus, *si neque Apostoli quidem Scripturas reliquissent.* This is that *regula fidei,* that *sacramentum symboli memoriæ mandatum,* of which St. Augustine says;—*noveritis hoc esse Fidei Catholicæ fundamentum super quod edificium surrexit Ecclesiæ.* This is the *norma Catholici et Ecclesiastici sensus,* determined and explicated, but not augmented, by the Nicene Fathers, as Waterland has rrefragably shown;—a norm or model of Faith grounded on the solemn affirmations of the Bishops collected from all parts of the Roman empire, that this was the essential and unalterable Gospel received by them from their predecessors in all the churches as the παράδοσις ἐκκλησιαστικὴ, *cui,* says Irenæus, *assentiunt multæ gentes eorum qui in Christum credunt sine charta et atramento, scriptam habentes per Spiritum in cordibus suis salutem, et veterum traditionem diligenter custodientes.* Let the attention of such as have been shaken by the assaults of Infidelity be thus directed, and then tell me wherein a spiritual physician would be blameworthy, if he carried on the cure by addressing his patient in this manner:—

"All men of learning, even learned unbelievers, admit that the greater part of the objections, urged in the popular works of Infidelity, to this or that verse or chapter of the Bible, prove only the ignorance or dishonesty of the objectors. But let it be supposed for a moment that a few remain hitherto unanswered,—nay, that to your judgment and feelings they appear unanswerable. What follows? That the Apostle's and Nicene Creed is not credible, the Ten Commandments not to be obeyed, the clauses of the Lord's Prayer not to be desired, or the Sermon on the Mount not to be practised?—See how the logic would look. David cruelly tortured the inhabitants of Rabbah (2 *Sam.* xii. 31; 1 *Chron.* xx. 3), and in several of the Psalms he invokes the bitterest curses on his enemies; therefore it is not to be believed that *the love of God toward us was manifested in sending his only-begotten Son into the world, that we might live through Him* (1 *John* iv. 9). Or: Abijah is said to have collected an army of 400,000 men, and Jeroboam to have met him with an army of 800,000, each army consisting of chosen men (2 *Chron.* xiii. 3), and making together a host of 1,200,000, and Abijah to have slain 500,000 out of the 800,000: therefore, the words which admonish us that *if God so loved us, we ought also to love one another* (1 *John* iv. 11), even our enemies, yea, *to bless them that curse us,* and to *do good to them that hate us* (*Matt.* v. 44), cannot proceed from the Holy Spirit. Or: The first six chapters of the Book of Daniel contain several words and phrases irreconcilable with the commonly received dates, and those chapters and the Book of Esther have a traditional and legendary character unlike that of the other historical books of the Old Testament: therefore, those other books, by contrast with which the former appear suspicious, and the historical document, 1 *Cor.* xv. 1—8, are not to be credited!"

We assuredly believe that the Bible contains all truths necessary to salvation, and that therein is preserved the undoubted Word of God. We assert likewise that, besides these express oracles and immediate revelations, there are Scriptures which to the soul and conscience of every Christian man bear irresistible evidence of the Divine Spirit assisting and actuating the authors; and that both these and the former are such as to render it morally impossible that any passage of the small inconsiderable portion, not included in one or other of these, can supply either ground or occasion of any error in faith, practice, or affection, except to those who wickedly and wilfully seek a pretext for their unbelief. And if in that small portion of the Bible which stands in no necessary connection with the known and especial ends and purposes of the Scriptures, there should be a few apparent errors resulting from the state of knowledge then existing—errors which the best and holiest men might entertain uninjured, and which without a miracle those men must have entertained; if I find no such miraculous prevention asserted, and see no reason for supposing it—may I not, to ease the scruples of a perplexed inquirer, venture to say to him: "Be it so. What then? The absolute infallibility even of the inspired writers in matters altogether incidental and foreign to the objects and purposes of their inspiration is no part of my Creed; and even if a professed divine should follow the doctrine of the Jewish Church so far as not to attribute to the *Hagiographa,* in every word and sentence, the same height and fulness of inspiration as to the Law and the Prophets, I feel no warrant to brand him as a heretic for an opinion, the admission of which disarms the Infidel without endangering a single article of the Catholic Faith.—If to an unlearned but earnest and thoughtful neighbour, I give the advice;—"Use the Old Testament to express the affections excited, and to confirm the faith and morals taught you, in the New, and leave all the rest to the students and professors of theology and Church history! You profess only to be a Christian:"—am I misleading my brother in Christ?

This I believe by my own dear experience,—that the more tranquilly an inquirer takes up the Bible as he would any other body of ancient writings, the livelier and steadier will be his impressions of its superiority to all other books, till at length all other books and all other knowledge will be valuable in his eyes in proportion as they help him to a better understanding of his Bible. Difficulty after difficulty has been overcome from the time that I began to study the Scriptures with free and unboding spirit, under the conviction that my faith in the Incarnate Word and his Gospel was secure, whatever the result might be;—the difficulties that still remain being so few and insignificant in my own estimation, that I have less personal interest in the question than many of those who will most dogmatically condemn me for presuming to make a question of it.

So much for scholars—for men of like education and pursuits as myself. With respect to Christians generally, I object to the consequence drawn from the Doctrine rather than to the Doctrine itself;—a consequence not only deducible from the premises, but actually and imperiously deduced; according to which every man that can but read is to sit down to the consecutive and connected perusal of the Bible under the expectation and assurance that the whole is within his comprehension, and that, unaided by note or comment, catechism or liturgical preparation, he is to find out for himself what he is bound to believe and practise, and that whatever he conscientiously understands by what he reads, is to be *his* religion. For he has found it in his Bible, and the Bible is the Religion of Protestants!

Would I then withhold the Bible from the Cottager and the Artisan? —Heaven forefend! The fairest flower that ever clomb up a cottage window is not so fair a sight to my eyes, as the Bible gleaming through the lower panes. Let it but be read as by such men it used to be read; when they came to it as to a ground covered with manna, even the bread which the Lord had given for his people to eat; where he that gathered much had nothing over, and he that gathered little had no lack. They gathered every man according to his eating. They came to it as to a treasure-house of Scriptures; each visitant taking what was precious and leaving as precious for others;—Yea, more, says our worthy old Church-historian, Fuller, where "the same man at several times may in his apprehension prefer several Scriptures as best, formerly most affected with one place, for the present more delighted with another, and afterwards, conceiving comfort therein not so clear, choose other places as more pregnant and pertinent to his purpose. Thus God orders it, that divers men, (and perhaps the same man at divers times) make use of all his gifts, gleaning and gathering comfort, as it is scattered through the whole field of the Scripture."

Farewell.

LETTER VII

You are now, my dear Friend, in possession of my whole mind on this point,—one thing only excepted which has weighed with me more than all the rest, and which I have therefore reserved for my concluding

Letter. This is the impelling principle, or way of thinking, which I have in most instances noticed in the assertors of what I have ventured to call Bibliolatry, and which I believe to be the main ground of its prevalence at this time, and among men whose religious views are anything rather than enthusiastic. And I here take occasion to declare, that my conviction of the danger and injury of this principle was and is my chief motive for bringing the Doctrine itself into question; the main error of which consists in the confounding of two distinct conceptions, revelation by the Eternal Word, and actuation of the Holy Spirit. The former indeed is not always or necessarily united with the latter—the prophecy of Balaam is an instance of the contrary,—but yet being ordinarily, and only not always, so united, the term, Inspiration, has acquired a double sense.

First, the term is used in the sense of Information miraculously communicated by voice or vision; and secondly, where without any sensible addition or infusion, the writer or speaker uses and applies his existing gifts of power and knowledge under the predisposing, aiding, and directing actuation of God's Holy Spirit. Now—between the first sense, that is, inspired revelation, and the highest degree of that grace and communion with the Spirit, which the Church under all circumstances, and every regenerate member of the Church of Christ, is permitted to hope, and instructed to pray for,—there is a positive difference of kind,—a chasm, the pretended overleaping of which constitutes imposture, or betrays insanity. Of the first kind are the Law and the Prophets, no jot or tittle of which can pass unfulfilled, and the substance and last interpretation of which passes not away; for they wrote of Christ, and shadowed out the everlasting Gospel. But with regard to the second, neither the holy writers—the so called *Hagiographi*—themselves, nor any fair interpretations of Scripture, assert any such absolute diversity or enjoin the belief of any greater difference of degree, than the experience of the Christian World, grounded on, and growing with, the comparison of these Scriptures with other works holden in honour by the Churches, has established. And *this* difference I admit; and doubt not that it has in every generation been rendered evident to as many as read these Scriptures under the gracious influence of the spirit in which they were written.

But alas! this is not sufficient; this cannot but be vague and unsufficing to those, with whom the Christian religion is wholly objective, to the exclusion of all its correspondent subjective. It must appear vague, I say, to those whose Christianity, as matter of belief, is wholly external, and, like the objects of sense, common to all alike;—altogether historical, an *opus operatum*,—its existing and present operancy in no respect differing from any other fact of history, and not at all modified by the supernatural principle in which it had its origin in time. Divines of this persuasion are actually, though without their own knowledge, in a state not dissimilar to that, into which the Latin Church sank deeper and deeper from the sixth to the fourteenth century; during which time religion was likewise merely objective and superstitious,—a letter proudly emblazoned and illuminated, but yet a dead letter that was to be read by its own outward glories without the light of the Spirit in the mind of the believer. The consequence was too glaring not to be anticipated, and, if possible, prevented. Without that spirit in each true believer, whereby we know the spirit of truth and the spirit of error in all things appertaining to salvation, the consequence must be—So many men, so many minds!—And what was the antidote which the Priests and Rabbis of this purely objective Faith opposed to this peril?—Why, an objective, outward Infallibility; concerning which, however, the differences were scarcely less or fewer than those which it was to heal;—an Infallibility, which, taken literally and unqualified, became the source of perplexity to the well-disposed, of unbelief to the wavering, and of scoff and triumph to the common enemy;—and which was, therefore, to be qualified and limited, and then it meant so much and so little, that to men of plain understandings and single hearts it meant nothing at all. It resided here. No! there. No! but in a third subject. Nay! neither here, nor there, nor in the third, but in all three conjointly!

But even this failed to satisfy; and what was the final resource,—the doctrine of those who would not be called a Protestant Church, but in which doctrine the Fathers of Protestantism in England would have found little other fault, than that it might be affirmed as truly of the decisions of any other Bishop as of the Bishop of Rome? The final resource was to restore what ought never to have been removed—the correspondent subjective, that is, the assent and confirmation of the Spirit promised to all true believers, as proved and manifested in the reception of such decision by the Church Universal in all its rightful members.

I comprise and conclude the sum of my conviction in this one sentence. Revealed Religion (and I know of no religion not revealed) is in its highest contemplation the unity, that is, the identity or coinherence, of Subjective and Objective. It is in itself, and irrelatively, at once inward Life and Truth, and outward Fact and Luminary. But as all Power manifests itself in the harmony of correspondent Opposites, each supposing and supporting the other,—so has Religion its objective, or historic and ecclesiastical pole, and its subjective, or spiritual and individual pole. In the miracles, and miraculous parts of religion— both in the first communication of divine truths, and in the promulgation of the truths thus communicated—we have the union of the two, that is, the subjective and supernatural displayed objectively—outwardly and phemonenally—*as* subjective and supernatural.

Lastly, in the Scriptures, as far as they are not included in the above as miracles, and in the mind of the believing and regenerate Reader and Meditater, there is proved to us the reciprocity, or reciprocation, of the Spirit as subjective and objective, which in conformity with the Scheme proposed by me, in aid of distinct conception and easy recollection, I have named the Indifference.[1] What I mean by this, a familiar acquaintance with the more popular parts of Luther's Works, especially his Commentaries, and the delightful volume of his Table Talk, would interpret for me better than I can do for myself. But I do my best, when I say that no Christian probationer, who is earnestly working out his salvation, and experiences the conflict of the spirit with the evil and the infirmity within him and around him, can find his own state brought before him and, as it were, antedated, in writings reverend even for their antiquity and enduring permanence, and far more, and more abundantly, consecrated by the reverence, love, and grateful testimonies of good men through the long succession of ages, in every generation, and under all states of minds and circumstances of fortune, —that no man, I say, can recognise his own inward experiences in such writings, and not find an objectiveness, a confirming and assuring

---

[1] "The Papacy elevated the Church to the virtual exclusion or suppression of the Scriptures; the modern Church of England, since Chillingworth, has so raised up the Scriptures as to annul the Church: both alike have quenched the Holy Spirit, as the *mesothesis* or indifference of the two, and substituted an alien compound for the genuine Preacher, which should be the *synthesis* of the Scriptures and the Church, and the sensible voice of the Holy Spirit."—*Lit. Rem.* vol. iii, p. 93.—*Ed.*

outwardness, and all the main characters of reality, reflected therefrom on the spirit, working in himself and in his own thoughts, emotions, and aspirations—warring against sin, and the motions of sin. The unsubstantial, insulated Self passes away as a stream; but these are the shadows and reflections of the Rock of Ages, and of the Tree of Life that starts forth from its side.

On the other hand, as much of reality, as much of objective truth, as the Scriptures communicate to the subjective experiences of the Believer, so much of present life, of living and effective import, do these experiences give to the letter of these Scriptures. In the one *the Spirit itself beareth witness with our spirit,* that we have received the *spirit of adoption*; in the other our spirit bears witness to the power of the Word, that it is indeed the Spirit that proceedeth from God. If in the holy men thus actuated all imperfection of knowledge, all participation in the mistakes and limits of their several ages had been excluded, how could these Writings be or become the history and example, the echo and more lustrous image of the work and warfare of the sanctifying Principle in us?—If after all this, and in spite of all this, some captious litigator should lay hold of a text here or there—St. Paul's *cloak left at Troas with Carpus,* of a verse from the Canticles, and ask: "Of what spiritual use is this?"—the answer is ready:—It proves to us that nothing can be so trifling as not to supply an evil heart with a pretext for unbelief.

Archbishop Leighton has observed that the Church has its extensive and intensive states, and that they seldom fall together. Certain it is, that since kings have been her nursing fathers, and queens her nursing mothers, our theologians seem to act in the spirit of fear rather than in that of faith; and too often instead of inquiring after the Truth in the confidence, that whatever is truth must be fruitful of good to all who *are in Him that is true,* they seek with vain precautions *to guard against the possible inferences* which perverse and distempered minds may pretend, whose whole Christianity,—do what we will—is and will remain nothing but a Pretence.

You have now my entire mind on this momentous Question, the grounds on which it rests, and the motives which induce me to make it known; and I now conclude by repeating my request—Correct me, or confirm me.

Farewell.

NOTE

"CONFESSIONS OF AN INQUIRING SPIRIT"

BY SARA COLERIDGE

"The main error of which" (ordinary doctrine of plenary inspiration) "consists in the confounding of two distinct conceptions, revelation by the Eternal Word, and actuation of the Holy Spirit. Between the first sense, that is, inspired revelation, and the highest degree of that grace and communion with the Spirit, which the Church under all circumstances, and every regenerate member of the Church of Christ, is permitted to hope, and instructed to pray, for—there is a positive difference of kind,—a charm, the pretended overleaping of which constitutes imposture, or betrays insanity. *Of the first kind are the Law and the Prophets, no jot or tittle of which can pass unfulfilled, and the substance and last interpretation of which passes not away; for they wrote of Christ, and shadowed out the everlasting Gospel.* But with regard to the second, neither the holy writers themselves, nor any fair interpretations of Scripture, assert any such absolute diversity, or enjoin the belief of any greater difference of degree than the experience of the Christian world, grounded on, and growing with, the comparison of these Scriptures with other works holden in honour by the Churches, has established."

"*But, alas! this is not sufficient: this cannot but be vague and unsufficing to those whose Christianity, as matter of belief, is wholly external, and, like the objects of sense, common to all alike, altogether historical, an* opus operatum.

"Does not the universally admitted canon—that each part of Scripture must be interpreted by the spirit of the whole—lead to the same practical conclusion as that for which I am now contending;—namely, that *it is the Spirit of the Bible, and not the detached words and sentences, that is infallible and absolute?*

"We assuredly believe that the Bible contains all truths necessary to salvation, and that therein is preserved the undoubted Word of God."

"Malice scorned, puts out
Itself, but argued, gives a kind of credit
To a false accusation."

A kind of credit may for a time accrue to falsehood from the very contest which it has seemed worthy to occasion; but, on the other hand, the prosecution of it—that is to say, its exposure by close and careful argument, may serve to the positive advancement of truth; more especially when the calumny relates to religious opinion, and has been prompted by the *odium theologicum*; since in such a case, the debate turns less upon personal matters, and more upon points by the consideration of which general principles and abstract rules of right and wrong are elucidated, than when facts of life and conduct, rather than opinions, are in question. All falsehood is mortal and perishable in its nature; yet mortal as it is, a sort of dying immortality or perpetuity of revivescence belongs to some particular delusions and forms of untruth. Lies so ancient that they date almost from the beginning, and were pierced with the arrows of Reasoning when the world was yet in its infancy, rise up from their graves, clad in new mail, like the dragons' teeth of Theban story, and come forth again to battle. Swarms of deceptions, which of old had been encountered by such sweeping blasts of contradiction, that they might be supposed as utterly extinct as the frogs and locusts that opened the doors of the House of Bondage, fly forth again to plague the world, showing their decease to have been but a stupefaction or winter sleep, like that of bats and swallows. Still, although falsehood perishes even when unassailed by those against whom it is directed; and comes to life again, after being put violently to death, it is not advisable always to leave it to the course of nature, or to refrain from pursuing it on account of its powers of resuscitation: Let us all in our day endeavour to combat untruth in every form in which it can appear, and leave the final event to the Father of Lights, from whom cometh every good and perfect gift of being and of knowing.

To apply these remarks. I have never doubted for a moment, that the accusation brought against this little work, namely, that it denies the Inspiration of Holy Scripture and undermines the faith in the Bible as the Word of God, must *put out itself* in proportion as the book is read with ordinary attention and intelligence; that it is even now dead for all who *have* read the book, and lives only for those who place implicit faith in the party organs whence it has proceeded, considering it a part of Christian zeal and prudence to keep on one side of all questions: to note and repeat every condemnatory sentence of their oracle, while they carefully refrain from communication with the condemned —the work pronounced heretical—lest it should perplex their minds by saying somewhat in its own behalf and exhibiting some contrariety to the vague and violent censure, which they have made up their minds to regard as an utterance of true piety and wisdom. The book is its own vindication; but the book cannot examine the strain of the accusatory discourse, detect the pernicious principle which it involves, or expose the unworthy means resorted to for the sake of accrediting it. There is the more inducement to this in the present instance, that so strong an example of superficial, deceptive, and at the same time for many minds, in a low condition of thought and feeling, persuasive argument as that to which I refer,—so perfect a specimen of morbid mental anatomy as it illustrates—is of rare occurrence; and as men are more vividly impressed by an exhibition of what has presented itself within the precincts of the actual, than by hypotheses and abstractions, however legitimate, and by strongly marked characters than by such as are faint and partial, I think that the mere display of the case will be sufficiently useful to justify the time and trouble it may cost to writer and reader.

The article in the "English Review" for December, 1848, entitled "Tendencies toward the Subversion of Faith," has, indeed, been already subjected to a severe and searching analysis by Archdeacon Hare and Mr. Maurice, in order to the refutation of its many injurious misstatements relative to themselves. To show how it has dealt with my Father, especially in regard to the *Confessions of an Inquiring Spirit*, will be but to complete that darkly faithful picture by filling up the background, which they have but slightly indicated, with its full measure of shadow. But let me present a general view of its design. The following method of crimination is adopted by the reviewer: a considerable number of writers, English and German, are brought into one most heterogeneous company, and on the alleged ground, that they all agree on a certain principle, or in certain sentiments concerning religious inquiry,—although it is confessed, because to conceal the fact would convict the writer of gross injustice even with the pliant and passive readers on whose sympathy he appears to calculate,—that on the most momentous questions which can agitate the mind of man they differ one among another *toto cælo*,—by the whole space of heaven—and if of heaven we may well be allowed to "couple hell,"—whatever infidel tendency can be discovered or imagined in the teaching of any one of the set is boldly attributed to all in common—as if the whole body of their opinions were one mass which must needs be leavened throughout with whatever poison is contained in any one individual's portion. It seems to be assumed by the reviewer, that the most dangerous opinions which belong to any of this arbitrarily formed band are the necessary results of the principle they all hold in common (that they all hold in common any such principle as that which he imputes to them is by no means to be allowed)—and on this plea the tendencies of those opinions and their consequences are coolly attributed to them all. By a similar process of reasoning we might discover Mahometan tendencies in all the great Fathers of the Church. St. Jerome, St. Austin, and St. Thomas Aquinas agreed with the author of the Koran, in condemning polytheism and idolatry—ergo, the opinions of Jerome, Augustine, and Aquinas tend the same way as those of Mahomet, namely, to the subversion of the doctrine of the cross and the divinity of Christ. Disbelief in a plurality of Gods may serve quite as well for a common indicator of religious tendencies as the principle which maintains the fitness of free inquiry in matters of faith. It might quite as rationally, and even more plausibly, be urged, that the Unity of the Godhead is a most dangerous tenet to insist upon, and must tend to the denial of the Incarnation, as that a man *must* be in the way to deny Revealed religion because he would have all men search the Scriptures for himself, search heaven and earth and his own heart and mind, the world without and the world within, by means of the faculties which God has given him, in order to the formation of his religious faith, and denies that submission to authority is the only principle on which he is to proceed in settling his religion. Socinus and the first Reformers, held in common, that Scripture binds the conscience only as interpreted by reason; that each individual must ultimately judge for himself, not only who and where are the true teachers of religion, but whether and how far their teaching is true. And the same notion is implied in the arguments of many of the ancient Fathers; ergo, the

Reformers and the ancient Fathers sought to undermine the Catholic belief in the divinity of Christ! A Papist indeed will readily adopt this inference, but can an English Reviewer afford to allow it? His own root principle, that it is unsafe not to rest the whole edifice of the faith on outward evidence, if common principles have the associative power ascribed to them in his argument, would bind him in close connection with the vilest and most degraded religions on the face of the earth; for the lower men are in the scale of intellect and feeling the more they rest on the sensuous and external, the more they look to see signs and wonders, and to hear the voice of multitudes giving testimony, in order to believe. Where can men look for proof and witness except in the sphere they know and are familiar with? They who cannot realise the spiritual to their apprehension, nor behold the invisible, cannot be expected to find evidences in the world of the spiritual and invisible.

To revert to the Anglican Inquisitor and his mode of discovering heresy and unbelief. Coleridge agreed with Blanco White, or Blanco White assented to the opinion of Coleridge, held by great divines before either of them saw the light, that "the main end of religion being the improvement of our nature and faculties, every part of religion is to be judged by its relation to this end;" or that the great test of the truth of a religion is its capability of evolving the highest faculties, and satisfying the highest requirements of the human mind; that reason, considered as a speculative power, not in its highest sense, as the fountain of ideas moral and spiritual, is to be "allowed the office in theology of determining on the negative truth of whatever we are required to believe!" therefore Coleridge's teaching tends the same way as that of Blanco White, namely to scepticism concerning the survival of personal consciousness after the dissolution of the body and a future state of weal or woe for the human soul! Now it must be admitted that Blanco White was not guarded from lapsing into a state of cheerless doubt or disbelief, and letting go from his "slack hand" the precious hopes of the Gospel, by the adoption of that maxim concerning the true test of religion, which has just been stated; but till the Reviewer has pointed out any religious principle, an intellectual assent to which will keep a man in the right way for evermore, he has certainly no right to assume that any which Blanco White held in common with Coleridge tends to the infidelity into which he fell towards the end of his life, in my belief from latent partial insanity; since bodily unsoundness is not unfrequently manifested in the form of mental disorder,—of pride, perverseness, causeless gloom, and impotence of religious faith and hope and joy in the Spirit. I mention the maxim above stated, although the Reviewer has not specified it, as being the most important on the theory of faith upon which they were of one mind. It *is* however specified in the article, that Blanco White "about 1825 formed a personal acquaintance with Coleridge, and on one occasion, paid a visit at his house six hours in length!" (at a time, let the reader observe, when he was by profession an orthodox Anglican;) nay more, that he and Mr. Coleridge afterwards wrote to each other! !—and these facts are adduced as proofs of a general affinity in their opinions, a oneness of tendency between them;—although Coleridge continued, to the end of his life, a zealous defender of the Trinity, which he held to be "the foundation of all rational theology;" "the one substantive truth, which is the form, manner, and involvent of all truths;" and thought there was "no medium between the Catholic Faith of Trinal Unity and Atheism disguised in the self-contradictory term, Pantheism;" while poor Blanco White was discovering that he had never really believed in the Trinity at all, and finally sinking from Socinianism into regular self-avowed disbelief of the Christian Revelation, or rather, finding that Socinianism *is,* logically developed, disbelief in a spiritual *Revelation,* even though it accepts the Scriptures as records of historic truth! Had the Reviewer looked for aught in the Memoir of Blanco White but weapons for his own illicit warfare, he must have seen that his latter correspondence contains no allusion to Coleridge or his views except one, and that in the form of a sneer intimating a peevish and unfounded suspicion—a suspicion evidently engendered by the *dispathy* produced in his mind by my Father's increasingly firm grasp of doctrines with respect to which his own mind was in a state of collapse—which, in this condition of feeble irritability, he had begun to regard with anger and a forced contempt.[1]

[1] The article speaks thus at p. 423: "To those who have perused Blanco White's life, the sympathy between Coleridge and him will not seem in the least surprising. They differed in details doubtless, because B. White rejected almost all the doctrines of Christianity in particular," (such minor and subordinate points, for instance, as the Trinity, the Incarnation, the spiritual effect of Sacraments, the Divinity of the Bible!) "But they were agreed in doubting or denying the Inspiration of the Word of God"—(What the truth of this assertion is in respect

It would hardly be credited, I think, that because my father was disposed to give German philosophy and theology a fair hearing, to winnow the sheaves of Teutonic thought before tying it in bundles to be burnt, or because he adopted the mental philosophy of Kant (—and who has ever yet out-argued that analysis of the pure reason, or the mind considered as the intellectual faculty apart from what it gains by experience—which he approved?—) because he even allowed some part of his reasonings in relation to theism, though only as hints and helps towards the detection of paralogisms in theology,—for the trial of untempered weapons which must bend or break in actual conflict—*therefore* he should be accused of sympathy with "such men as Strauss," whose book he never saw, and of whose hypothesis for solving the problem of Christianity, he was, by anticipation, a most zealous, I think I may add a very successful opponent! Or that because he had at one time intercourse with B. White, and strove to infuse into him truly philosophical and Catholic views, he should be set forth as a kindred spirit with that "most unhappy man of men," unhappy in the constitution of his mind and in its circumstances, who, however, spite of the blindness that came upon him respecting the divinity of Christ and a personal resurrection, preserved a faith in the one Supreme Being—a sense of fealty and unconditional submission to Him, as the Creator and Moral Governor of the world, I doubt not vastly more sincere and sustaining than that of numbers who think they do God service by transforming his doctrine into Atheism, and conforming his life and morals to their view of his opinions.[1] There are many

to Coleridge, let the reader judge)—"and their studies were directed to the same sources. The German philosophers and writers on religious subjects (we cannot bear to call them theologians), such as Kant, Fichte, Schleiermacher, Strauss, Nitsch, Neander, Paulus, &c., were especial objects of admiration to B. White, just as they were to Coleridge, and to his disciples, Mr. Hare and Mr. Sterling."

[1] TO JOSEPH BLANCO WHITE

Could'st thou so calmly, tried one, yield thy breath
Void of the Christian's sure and certain hope?
Didst thou to earth confine our being's scope,
Yet fix'd on One Supreme with fervent faith,
As though intent t' escape eternal scath,
Shun the smooth worldly ways that hell-ward slope?
O thou light-searching spirit that didst grope
In such bleak shadows here, 'twixt life and death,
For thee have I borne witness, though in ruth,

thoughtful men who declare that they were diverted from such notions as those of Strauss, from Deism more or less masked and disguised, by the teaching of Coleridge, when the divinity of the Reviewer's school of thought, "dry as the desert sands," or of Church Methodists, "unstable as water," might have driven them in that direction, or any direction opposite to the plainly irrational and utterly heartless.

The Reviewer himself would hardly fail to perceive the iniquity of his mode of inferring and concluding, if he found it applied to any but objects, the sight of whom excites his party feelings, so as to cover him with cloudy mists of passion. Let us suppose that some distinguished writer, who joins hand and heart with him against Wesleyanism on the one hand, and "Germanism" on the other, were accused of treachery to the Church in whose bosom he had been nurtured and is still nourished, simply because zealots of Ultra-Montanism in France mentioned him *with high respect*, or Italian Ecclesiastics condescended to admit that he *wrote like a Catholic.* Were such an inference drawn, even respecting one who walked somewhat nearer to Rome than the English Reviewer himself considered wise or safe, would he not indignantly reply, that the books of this writer were before the world, and so long as it is impossible, *out of them,* to convict him of teaching in a spirit contrary to his engagements and position in a Reformed Church, so long we ought to suppose his conscience void of reproach, and his conduct in religion conformed to those same rules of honesty and of honour which every good man observes in his general walk? Would he not think it shameful to breathe suspicion against such a man on the ground of a partial sympathy, or by reason of what other men think or pretend to have discovered in his writings? Which of my father's assailants, who strive to fasten on him a character of infidelity, and to set up a beacon of warning against his books, ever dared to lay hold of him in the Temple of his own Christian philosophy? Which of them has examined his system at large, or even fairly stated with due regard to what came before and followed after, any one of the particular passages, which have been cited as evidence of *tendencies to subvert the faith?* Who that has once fairly entered his struc-

> Like thee by blame unmoved—dare hope and pray
> That thou, released from that ill frame of clay,
> Thine earth-born clog, renew'd in heavenly youth,
> Mayst find that bliss untold, 'mid endless day,
> Awaits each earnest soul that lived for Truth.—S. C.

ture of thought and opinion, so grand in its ground plan, so exquisitely finished in parts, would accuse him of any disposition to undermine the Faith in a Spiritual Religion? He examined what are commonly called, among orthodox writers, the walls and foundations of the Faith in Christ, thought portions of them unsound, and most of them put to an important purpose to which, of themselves, they are unequal. His procedure is open and manifest—he threw out no suspicions against any doctrine without an explicit statement of the grounds of his doubts, —he never sought to convey an opinion into the minds of readers by addresses to the sensuous fancy, false analogies and visible images, the mockery of ideas; as showmen paint fancy monsters on the outside of their booths to prepossess beholders with the exciting character of what is within; and it is a question, whether any man, who really evoked the powers of thought, and addressed the higher and purer faculties of man's nature, ever led a studious and attentive reader finally away from truth, which he might otherwise have embraced sincerely and effectively.

He would, indeed, have denied, what the Reviewer asserts, that a belief in the plenary inspiration of Holy Writ, *understood in the ordinary sense,* is the only "rational foundation of his own belief" in Christianity. He would have maintained first, that such never has been, and by the nature of the human mind and of the truths in question, never can be, the ground of any vital saving belief in Redemption by Christ, the Incarnation of a Saviour truly God, the Aids of the Spirit, and a personal Resurrection of the entire man. That if these spiritual verities were not apprehensible by the *human,* though actuated and inspired, minds of the first teachers of the Gospel, neither could they be fitted to regenerate the minds of disciples,—to raise, to purify, to justify through *faith*—the true beatific vision upon earth. That if they were not "adapted to the needs and capabilities" of our "human nature," consequently proved divine by their divine fruits, the moral and spiritual effects visible to the moral and spiritual eye throughout the domains of the Gospel, no other species of proof would accredit them as the religion of a race gradually increasing in power of thought, the heirs of an estate and property of knowledge and intelligence accumulating from age to age. That if they were not attested by the voice of Christendom, echoed from generation to generation, no other kind of testimony would avail to make men Christians in faith and practice, though it might serve to make dull and obstinate men bigots and even persecutors in behalf of an hereditary creed. All this evidence is entirely independent of belief in plenary inspiration of Holy Writ, understood in the same sense against which my father contended; all this is indispensable, and where this is, a belief that all the Sacred Writers, in all they wrote, were guarded absolutely from error, may well be dispensed with.

Why did not the Reviewer state his inquisition principle boldly and plainly at once, and place it, so stated in the front of his article ? Why did he not plainly say (what his reasoning, if it have any coherency, implies), neither more nor less than this : Every man, who maintains that saving faith cannot be determined by one man for another, or that a man must see with the eyes of his own mind every spiritual reality which is to bless him here and bring him finally to a higher state of blessedness than can be enjoyed in the tabernacle of the flesh—every man who declares the Bible to be its own evidence, and that the perception—(whether it ever becomes the object of abstract contemplation and reflection or no, but at least the perception—) of this evidence is indispensable to its efficacy in educating the soul ; or in other words, that the great substantiative Revelation without which the outward one is a cold and empty outline, is that of the heart and spirit—every man who maintains that although the individual can be benefited by religious inquiry only as it is proportioned to his native powers, his means and opportunities, yet that speculation at large must be free, not restrained by a certain official body, who are to say to the ocean of human thought, So far shalt thou go and no farther, and here shall thy proud waves be stayed; that, whatever may be the interests of an ecclesiastico-political despotism, true religion can never be served by popish interdictions and suppressions, but the more widely the realm of thought is extended, the wider and hence the firmer may the foundations of faith be laid—is a traitor to the cause of God, and *must*, however spiritual his doctrines may appear, in all he teaches be tending to undermine a sure belief in Christianity? But no! such an enunciation from the first—such a display in full daylight of his argumentative machinery, would have been superfluous for the readers he reckoned on, and would have tended, if it had any effect at all, to defeat the object of the article. *For it would have awakened reflection.* Far better was his purpose served by playing before the eyes of readers little images of falsified facts, apart from their causes and occasions—appearances of links and connections between the various writers whom it was desired to bring into one common condemnation—links and connections between one and another, *at a particular time and for a particular object,* being exhibited, apart from their conditions and circumstances, as uniting the religious mind of some party at one end of the row with the blank infidelity of another party at the extreme opposite end—the *Christian* philosophy of the former with the Anti-Christian philosophy of the latter,—the qualification of Christian and Anti-Christian being quietly suppressed as unimportant to the examination!

> "Veramente più volte appajon cose,
> Che danno a dubitar falsa matera
> Per le vere cagion, che son nascose."

Letters pass—an interview takes place—influence is exercised—intercourse is carried on by some of the parties—some give their suffrages the same way in support of an obnoxious writer, who never appeared on the areana of controversy till one who, as the oldest, bears the chief weight of the general accusation, was dead—all these items of outward action and commonplaces of gossip are paraded before the eye of the reader like so many shreds from the Rag-fair of Lack-reason and Poverty of Thought. Thus the careless and ill-disposed are amused and confirmed in their prejudices, and hold themselves fully authorised to speak of all the writers named in the Review, doubtless with the omission of even the Reviewer's admissions in favour of some of them, as propagators of Infidelity and covert Atheism. There is no attempt throughout the article to examine any part of the teaching of the accused parties, unless the citation of a passage quite sure to mislead an uninformed reader as to the main drift of the work in which it occurs, if presented *without* its context and *with* the Reviewer's commentary, can be called such. The whole process consists in the collocation of extrinsic marks and symptoms—inferences at second hand to warrant conclusions the most comprehensive and stringent that one human being can draw against another in respect of his frame of religious thought and opinion. A more undisguised appeal to ignorant zealotry and unreflecting prejudice, or as Mr. Maurice expresses it, "to all the bitterness, hardness, and cruelty, which are in the English religious mind, above all to the sense which there is in that mind of the necessity of cleaving to some sect or system of opinions, because it has so feeble a hold on the eternal truths which the Bible and the Creeds set forth,"—although, from particular circumstances, my attention has been a good deal drawn to the Base Arts of Periodical Literature—it was never my lot to examine.

In reality the only thing common to the writers whom the Reviewer packs together, is, that they all, though with positive views of their own the most various and diverse, agree in negativing such views of faith as he and his school rely upon—in holding them to be in a religious sense already *nothing*. This is the true unity amongst them, and he would have done himself more justice, in respect of coherency of thought, if he could have afforded to state his real ground of disapproval and apprehension, instead of confounding oppugnancy to his religious opinions with hostility and resistance to the Divine light. He has indeed some reason to dislike and dread the author of the Aids to Reflection; his system *is* in danger from that and every other work which leads men to think on what they are required to believe. The writers he assails are unanimous in counteracting *him,* or at least such opinions as those he strives to uphold; he therefore would represent them as equally one in co-operating with the Prince of Darkness—with the Spirit of Infidelity and Rebellion against God. He should have reflected, before he published so many fearful charges, as Archdeacon Hare says of those against himself, and as I can say of those against my father, "without a tittle of evidence," and capable, as has been shown of direct disproof, whether he has any good right to place himself in such direct antithesis to him who was an injurious falsifier from the beginning; whether in his eager desire to maintain what, in his positiveness rather than certainty, (for Certainty brings proper proof, while Positiveness, like the article, only assumes and asserts,) he identifies with the cause of the Gospel, he is not joining hands with those who are ready to cheat and deceive in furtherance of their own opinion, and to vent half-truths which are in effect whole falsehoods of the grossest kind. Lucifer from the highest Angel passed mysteriously into a Devil, and in this ambiguous transitional stage of his existence perhaps it was that he begat the subtle fiend Lying for God—the most specious and bright-seeming emissary of the Pit, who conceals a dark distorted body beneath robes of light and "wings of sky-tinctured grain."

The Reviewer's general charge may, however, be *translated* into truth—into what is really and wholly true. "Tendencies toward the subversion of *Faith*." Let Faith be defined in accordance with the notions implied in the review, and we may readily admit the justness of the allegation. It is distinctive of the Writer's school to speak as if faith consisted in the admission of religious *credenda*, without any reference to their internal credibility for the mind that admits them, on authority and alleged proof from without. Historical testimony, or rather what passes for such with an influential majority, is, in their system, not merely *a* bulwark or buttress of religion, but *the* rock upon which it rests. Faith with them is not a spiritual intuition—the substance of things hoped for and evidence of things unseen with the bodily eye—but an assent to some truth which is, or may be, utterly unperceived by the eye of the mind, on a system of evidences of which the logical understanding alone is to judge. Is this that spiritual principle to which Scripture ascribes the power of saving the soul by purifying the heart? Can such blind submission be by any essential mark plainly distinguished from that abject credulity and obstinate adherence of spirit to articles obtruded by a self-asserting authority,[1] which may be

---

[1] The grand argument for the Papal Infallibility with some eminent and experienced Romish controversialists is simply this, that *such Infallibility is pretended to*. The principal reason they allege for maintaining the Church of Rome to be *the* true Church, out of which there is no salvation—to which alone the promises of Christ belong—is merely that *she claims to be the true Church.*—declares herself in possession of the Spirit of Truth, and the power of working miracles. This is a bold way of illustrating the Scriptural precept, *ask and ye shall receive—knock and it shall be opened unto you.* Rome has but to ask belief in her signs and wonders, to set forth pitiable and revolting forms of disease in some of her members as images of our Lord's awful wounds, or to set up the ancient dust of a cemetery as a sacred receptacle of the Saviour's overflowing virtue, accredited by a couple of dreamers, and straightway crowds celebrate the miserable miracle and bestow their offerings at the shrine of the manufactured martyr and saint. The Pope has but to *sit as God showing himself that he is God*, to make the high altar his *footstool*, and receive the adoration of his Cardinals! to exalt the Blessed Mary (doubtless to her own grief and horror, were she now susceptible of aught but blessedness,) into a new *Bruiser of the Serpent's Head*, a secondary and as it were vicegerent Redeemer, *the Intercessor betwixt Christ and His Church*, that is to say between God and Man—to make a new Door of the Sheepfold—open out a new fountain *of all hope, grace, and salvation*—to claim to be himself a delegated Saviour, the Head of the Church upon earth!—Such arrogations are quite sufficient to subdue the mind of multitudes—and indeed the maintainers of

found in union with the most debased and abominable superstitions, the lowest and most impure code of morals? It is not to be denied that the writers in question, those to whom the Reviewer allows most orthodoxy, more distinctly and earnestly perhaps than those whom he places at the bottom of the list in point of right belief, have laboured toward the subversion of such a *faith* as this, or rather such a theory concerning the faith that is to save the soul. I fully believe that they and others following in their steps will succeed in overthrowing that confidence in the sole sufficiency of what has commonly been received as outward evidence, and in the danger and folly of applying other deeper tests of the truth, and will thereby strengthen the faith in Christ, by bringing into prominence the only ground which is strong enough and wide enough to bear a structure intended for immortality. So long as men fancy, without examination, that there is an array of evidences amply sufficient *per se* to secure the whole body of the faith, they will feel little inducement to examine what security is contained in the articles themselves, or to hold them in that truth which alone can endure. Their very dread of argument and investigation is a plain proof that the school in question has no such insight, and therefore no such ground of confidence. They who feel the divinity of the Bible as a whole, to be a truth no more to be gainsaid by a spiritually sane mind than the blue face of the heavens can be discoloured and lose its azure for the sound and healthful eye, however the patient afflicted with acyanoblepsia may report of it, will entertain no dread of criticism or metaphysical investigations imported from Germany or elsewhere, however they may dissent from the conclusions of particular investigators. The *Idea* of a divine Redeemer cannot be *argued* away; upon the

implicit faith and uninquiring submission to authority seem to be quite in a false position when they set at nought those of the Papacy. If any reader is startled, and inclined to doubt what I have repeated concerning the Virgin Mary, I refer him to the Pope's last Encyclical Letter; for confirmation of what I have said about the Pope's *setting his feet on the Altar,* let him read Dr. Wordsworth's exposure of the Church of Rome in his admirable *Letters to Gondon,* and consult the authorities to which he there refers. His account of the inauguration of a Pope must make any but the slaves of Rome or her thorough-paced admirers shudder; but, shocking as such practical blasphemy must appear to all else, I believe it to be excellent *policy,* supreme wisdom in reference to this world and its generations. The loftier are the pretension of ecclesiastical usurpers, even if they outsoar those which the plain of Shinar witnessed of old, the greater will be their success. In this fearful sense is the kingdom of heaven daily taken by violence in the modern Babylon.

degree of power with which this is evolved from within,—and realised by the submission of the practical life to its influence, depends the faith in Holy Scripture. To those who behold this Idea vividly, and are possessed by it, the New Testament will ever appear true history— the Old will be received in such a spirit as deep belief in the Gospel necessitates. Kant speaks in his Preface to the *Kritik der reinen Vernunft*, of the "ridiculous despotism of the schools"—how they "raise a loud cry about public danger when their spiders' webs are pulled to pieces, of which webs the public had never taken notice and the loss of which it can never feel." That theory of belief or of theological profession, which the Reviewer so zealously guards, identifying any danger in which free inquiry may place it with jeopardy of *the Faith*, is a human tissue that may be rent, I trust, without peril to Christianity, which never has been sustained on any other foundation than that of its intrinsic worth and credibility, attested by its visible spiritual fruits.

A belief, however true and pure, which is held without being spiritually apprehended is but a talent of gold wrapped in a napkin. If it be spiritually apprehended, this proof of its truth must be far before, even if it do not supersede, every other. I say *spiritually* apprehended, for doubtless a distinction must be made betwixt the power to exhibit a doctrine in an exact philosophical formula, or to show its accordance with speculative reason, and that of beholding, or beneficially possessing, the idea which forms its life and substance. For the Church at large a consistent dogmatic system distinctly drawn out is necessary; but this wall of fortification need not surround every private dwelling, every one of the many mansions in the great House of the Spirit.

But let me give the very words in which the Reviewer states the principle that unites, according to his judgment, so many dissimilar and mutually opposed thinkers in the common service of infidelity. "What is the common characteristic of that school? We believe it to consist simply in the striving after intellectual liberty," (to desire the bondage of the intellect therefore, is in his opinion, the only religious attitude of mind;) "a tendency to reject all which does not commend itself to the individual reason as right and true—a tendency to resist authority, of whatever nature it may be, which interposes any restraint on the freedom of speculation. It is not so much any objective truth, which thinkers of this class contend for, as liberty of thought in general. Their objection is not to individual doctrines, but to any supposed obligation on individuals to receive those doctrines." This vague but sweeping charge may receive two precise interpretations, the one totally different from the other—the one involving principles that must overturn all settled belief in revealed religion, while the other is the exponent of such as are absolutely necessary to the holding of religious belief truthfully, intelligently, therefore effectively and securely. Will the author dare to construe it thus?— the writers in question, one and all of them, deny that there is any objective reality independent of the human mind, of supreme interest to the individual, which does not at all times appear such to his individual mind, whatever be his means and opportunities of coming to the knowledge of the truth, whatever, from the use of his will, the use he may make of them; they hold it right to disregard all outward testimony that may be alleged, all the impressions, convictions, reasonings of other minds that can serve to guide and to modify the results of religious meditation; to set aside all consideration of the consentient feelings and belief of the lights of the world from age to age? Will he dare, I say, to construe the charge thus, and to bring it thus construed to bear upon the author of the Aids to Reflection, the Lay Sermons, the Friend, and the Letters on Inspiration? My Father, from the time that he rose out of the suspense and uncertainty as to his theological system, which caused him to seek, for awhile, a recess with the Unitarians, (whom he found, however, quite as dogmatic in their narrow creed as the Church in her wider one,)—when the elements of Faith were for his mind in a sort of chaos that was yet to be shaped by Reason, divinely illumined, into a spiritual world, —from this time forth was a defender of historical Christianity, and as such of course of appropriate historical testimony and proof, although, for reasons which neither the Reviewer nor any other assailant has ever attempted to rebut, he considered this secondary and subordinate in the system of evidence, and dependent, in a great degree, for its cogency and persuasiveness on the intrinsic character of the great vital spiritualities which the religious history represents as objectively realised. He doubtless sometimes sought to demonstrate the weakness of alleged authority and testimony in particular instances; but on the subject of authority and testimony at large, his principles are in accordance with those of the great Christian Doctors and Fathers and Philosophers from the beginning of the Christian æra to the present day.

But the accusation may be reduced to truth under the following form: the accused are guilty of holding that no man receives spiritual benefit from any doctrine which he does not apprehend by the spirit within him; that a belief so held, however pure and true in itself, is but as the talent of gold folded in a napkin, and instead of purifying the heart, may lie side by side in the treasury of the mind with the most abject superstitions and lowest moral perceptions; that a theological formula, like that of *con* or *trans*-substantiation, which cannot be proved consistent with itself and with the laws of thought, is a nullity and can be no *proper exponent* of a spiritual truth, although a spiritual truth may be arbitrarily united with it: that the formal statement of a doctrine being its body, without which it cannot be organised so as to become a living moving reality, it must be injured in its internal being, and impeded in its free motions, by such imprisonment, and be in constant danger of extinction.

Mr. Coleridge rejects no belief, which has prevailed in the Church, without considering all that is alleged on its behalf of every kind of testimony. But if a doctrine appears to be self-contradictory and devoid of spiritual significancy, if the maintainers of the tenet cannot themselves disprove the charge that it obtrudes upon the mind a visual image to which no spiritual idea corresponds, which cannot be ex-changed for aught of value in the world of super-sensual reality, that image being a mere fabric of the brain, like the visions of poets or romancers, (more truly indeed than they, as the visions of good poets always represent a truth), are we bound to acquiesce in it by force of any outward proof or testimony that has ever yet been alleged in support of particular views in theology?

The Romanist, in accordance with the policy of his Church system, demands of course that every doctrine should be implicitly received, without regard to its internal character. Yet a voice which even his system cannot stifle, with a whisper clearly audible in the lull of theo-logical dogmatising, urges him to justify his belief, if possible, in the Court of Reason and the Spiritual Sense: to show that it is not self-contradictory—that it does represent a spiritual reality. He alleges that, in the Lord's Supper, there is a change of *substance*, the accidents of bread and wine remaining unchanged. This reasoning he puts forth,

7

requiring you however not to exercise your reasoning faculty upon it;—which is as reasonable a procedure as if one should offer to cheer the heart of the sinking wayfarer, by pouring wine into his cup, at the same time forbidding him to drink, lest he should discover, in the process of swallowing, that it is not wine but water dyed red with some deleterious ingredient, that has been charitably bestowed upon him; or as if one should give a starving beggar counters for coin, enjoining him not to deal with them, lest he should find that they are not good money, and have no currency. To enjoy a religious truth is indeed something more than to subject it to intellectual analysis; but I think it may be affirmed, that a tenet, which will not endure this process, is no vehicle of a spiritual truth and substance by which the simple may be nourished to eternal life. Believing thus, we who have not delivered ourselves up blindfold to any self-asserted church upon earth, assured that the Divine Light, even Christ Jesus, who ever referred man to his innate powers of receiving and perceiving heavenly truth, owns no church that demands, and is satisfied with, implicit faith,—will venture to examine the pretended wine—the so-called coin of value. We will venture to ask what is the sense or signification of the saying, that the accidents of bread are to be found apart from the substance of bread, and that the substance of flesh, apart from the accidents of flesh, supports the accidents of bread? The accidents of bread, taken together with whatsoever it is that constitutes their unity or makes them to be one thing, are *what we mean by the word bread,* neither more nor less; and to affirm that bread can be absent where its accidents are present, and that flesh can be where the accidents or sensuous *phœno-mena* of flesh are not, what is it but to affirm and deny in one and the same proposition? All that we *mean* by bread is present in the elements after consecration as before, and all that we *mean* by flesh is absent. The substance of bread is neither more nor less than whatsoever stands under—*sub stat*—the accidents, or sensuous appearances, of bread. If it be asked, how is this proved? I reply, it has been demonstrated by a metaphysical deduction, which has never yet been invalidated, that the term (substance) is a mere form of the intellect which expresses the unity of any particular external object. We can become cognisant only of that which is presented to us by our faculties of sense, or which the mind perceives within itself. What *reason* can we have to believe that there is anything in this or that object beyond what meets our senses and the connection of it into one thing by a mental act? If there *were* anything beyond this, we have no power of ascertaining it. To say therefore that the substance of one thing can be under the accidents of another thing, as if *substance,* instead of being a mere relative term, expressing the unity of any *congeries of phænomena,* were a self-subsisting independent reality, which could be abstracted from that to which it relates,—that the substance of a material object can exist apart from all accidents, determinations, or modes of being, and can be transferred from one set of modes or determinations to another; just as a pedestal may be removed from under that which it supports, and placed under another object; is really as absurd as to imply that a subject can exist without a predicate, and a predicate without a subject— or that we might conceive North apart from South, or, extinguishing the West, might yet retain the East, as an intelligible term, in the description of the realms of Space.

Our Saviour in his miracles appealed to the senses of beholders for the proof of the sensuous transformation; but these dealers in signs and wonders, the priests of Rome, proclaim a supernatural, sensuous, or at least material, change to which our senses can bear no witness. They who maintain the *real presence* to be the substance or substrate of the flesh and blood of our Lord's body under the material accidents of bread and wine, plainly hold the dogma in that "gross corporeal sense" which Mr. Newman, when he wrote Tract ninety, abjured. Your thorough Romanist is dissatisfied unless it be confessed that the flesh of our Lord's body, which was seen and handled eighteen hundred years ago, is present under the *phænomena* of bread. A real presence of the whole undivided Christ, divine and human, soul and supersensuous body, to the entire man of every devout receiver,—this sublime and *substantial* belief seems to them, in their grovelling fanaticism, a thin impalpable shade, a mockery, a rationalistic subterfuge. *The gross and sensible is alone, to their minds, the substantial.* They are unable to breathe the thin air at the mountain summit of a philosophical and spiritual faith. But it is vain to argue against a reasonless and irrational creed with those who make it their boast that they neither deny, nor even suspend their assent to, articles, however in themselves indefensible, if they be but commended to them by what their reasoning and concluding faculty has decided to be sufficient authority. It is natural enough, in the sphere they inhabit, wherein "imposture, organised into a comprehensive and self-consistent whole, forms a world of its own, in which inversion is the order of nature"— it is natural enough in such a sphere, wherein "all forms of sophistry are native," that the most unnatural creed should appear the most worthy of belief; and that the saying of Tertullian should be taken, not in Tertullian's excellent sense, but in its literal senselessness:—*Prorsus credible est quia ineptum est ;—certum est quia impossibile.*[1]

I believe, however, it may be shown that consubstantiation, as taught by some of our Anglican divines, is as empty a doctrine as the dogma insisted on by the Council of Trent: that what this tenet asserts *beyond* and *in distinction from,* the doctrine of the Real Presence as taught by Hooker, namely that Christ Himself is present to the spirit of the faithful receiver of the sacrament duly administered, is equally devoid of spiritual content. What is the meaning of the word *presence* when applied to a thing of spirit? A material object is *present* to man when it is near enough in space to his material organism to be apprehended by his outward senses. A spiritual object cannot be *present* in this way. Considered in itself, it has no relations of space. Spirit is *present* either to spirit or to matter by acting or operating upon it,—by producing certain effects. A spiritual power is present to material things by causing certain material results; it is thus we understand the presence of God in the Material Universe. The Divine Spirit maintains in life the whole frame of visible things, and is, in this sense, the *Anima Mundi.* Jehovah was said to be *present* in the burning bush, and in the Shechinah within the Holy of Holies. What does this mean but that the Lord caused visible tokens to appear in particular places in order to assure the hearts of believers, to signify to them that they were under an extraordinary Providence, or that their prayers should be answered. But this proves nothing with respect to the Being of God Himself. God Himself is not in the Temple made with hands, or nigh the altar, or on the table of divine communion, except as He is everywhere. But man in his human frame is present in particular places; and God in his converse with man addresses him in his own language, conforms Himself to his faculties. It will hardly be affirmed that the words *This is my body*, must needs be taken in a literal sense; that the expression may not be figurative, while the import is real and substantial; namely, this is that whereby the power of my humanity

[1] De Carne Christi, cap. v.

shall be operative in your spirits, nourishing your souls and bodies to eternal life; *this is my body in power and operation*: the effect being put for the cause by a common form of rhetoric.

So again to affirm that, in the moment of baptism, the soul of an infant is spiritually changed, without any intuition of divine truth by the eye of the spirit within him, or submission of his will to the will of God, and that this is that regeneration of which our Lord spake to Nicodemus, which His Apostle John describes in his first Epistle General,—is not this to say and unsay in a breath? What means *spiritual regeneration* but a general change in the spirit wrought by the Spirit of Holiness? What is the spirit of man but his rational will, or moral and intelligential being? And how can this change, represented by our Lord and his Apostle as the ground of conversion, and consequently of eternal life and salvation, be predicated of an infant, whose reason and will are yet latent and inactive, who, after the sacrament, not only remains liable to sin mortally, but who may, as soon as his moral being is developed, discover none but evil propensities, and neglect all opportunities of grace and salvation? In the vegetable world, a vigorous germ may be prevented from due growth and expansion by circumstances of soil and season, or it may be destroyed mechanically by impact from without, by the crushing foot, the falling stone, or gnawing insect. But this oft alleged analogy has no real application here. The spiritual power, a reception whereof constitutes the new birth, is essentially a power to resist temptation, or, in Scripture phrase, to *overcome the world*. A regenerate person cannot be corrupted by ill education; *he is well educated by the Spirit already, in that he is regenerate*.

Holy Scripture describes the new birth as a moral and religious general renovation, constituting the subject of it *a new creature*. Maintainers of the mystic momentary dogma affirm that this is regeneration *viewed in its results*,—regeneration with all the effects it produces when the soul has been enlightened by Light from above and the will has submitted to the leading of the Spirit. But what authorises us to say, that such a moral and spiritual condition, as is identified in the New Testament with regeneration, is the *result* of a supposed mystical change, which may be totally inoperative? It is the immediate operation of the Holy Spirit upon man's spirit which produces holiness and fitness for Heaven; and if, after baptism, the heart and mind and moral being may remain unsanctified,—unaffected for good by the supposed change,—how can we reasonably ascribe to this imaginary font-renewal—this visionary clothing of the soul in spirit-robes of perfect whiteness—all that actualised faith and positive evil-overcoming holiness on which the Blessed Evangelist expatiates? Obviously this font-renewal by itself does not affect the moral being at all. How then can it be the source and parent of a blessed trans-naturation of the whole heart and mind, enduing the subject of it with eternal life?

Once more, what is the *sense* of dæmoniac possession, as commonly understood? Can one personal identity or distinct self-subsisting spirit enter into, or become commingled with, another distinct personal being, as Jonah entered into the body of the whale, or as leaven can diffuse itself through a measure of meal? If the supposition is that the dæmon does but enter the *body* or outward phenomenal organism of the afflicted person, so that *pro tempore* there are two souls to one body, how can it be said that, in such a case, the *man* is possessed, or how does this answer to the notion of the subject commonly entertained, which is, undoubtedly, that the *soul* of the dæmoniac is the seat of the dæmon? Inspiration of Satan, or his agents and underlings, is as obviously a different conception from the popular one, which imports not merely that an Evil Spirit *acts upon* the soul, then ceases to act upon it, but that a personal Evil Being *occupies* the soul and afterwards is literally cast *out* of it. But then our Lord spoke as if the matter were as it is popularly represented. I answer, why must our Lord have combated vulgar errors in psychology and nosology and physics, or explained scientifically the nature of madness to unprepared minds, any more than anticipated the teaching of Bacon and of Newton? Not only was this unnecessary—it would directly and positively have interfered with the great spiritual objects of his mission. We may well believe that, in transferring the disorder of a maniac to a herd of swine, unlawfully bred and retained, He may have adopted the prevailing notions, made use of the ordinary language of the time and country in which He appeared ,without derogating from his divine perfections, or affecting in the least degree his transcendent character as the Way and the *Truth*, the *Light* as well as the Life of Men. There are some other such empty husks in the basket of popular theology;—but to return to our Conservative, and his accusation against certain modern Reformers of theological thought:

"It is not so much any objective truth which thinkers of this class contend for as liberty of thought in general. Their objection is not to individual doctrines, but to any supposed obligation on individuals to receive those doctrines." An attentive perusal of the Aids to Reflection would convince any reasonable person that the author *contended for a whole body* of objective truth, and most carefully distinguished the mere subjective forms of religious thought, which are not binding on the conscience because they are merely subjective, however legitimate and self-consistent, from those verities which the outward Revelation, in its accordance with that of the heart and spirit, enlightened from above, has realised: that if he contended for liberty of thought he duly guarded against licence or licentiousness, and demanded that speculation might be free in order that it might be full—powerful to the reception of spiritual riches, as they alone whose hands are unfettered can gather in the Harvest. Where has he ever denied, directly or by implication, that it is not obligatory on man to receive objective truth when presented to him? To deny this indeed would be to cast confusion on the face of the Bible, in which faith is represented as *duty*, while at the same time it is declared that faith comes by hearing and knowledge of the truth, which proves it to be no vague impulse distinct from any exercise of reason. They who rely on outward evidence alone, and decry as *rationalism* the belief that a perception of the *reasonableness* of what we are required to believe is the deepest ground of faith, place the proof of religion out of the sphere of the will, the heart and moral being, confining it within the precincts of the understanding, which alone judges of the outward proof. Such reasoners cannot consistently describe faith as duty: in my Father's system faith is at once a *light, a beholding of truth*, and "the source and sum, the energy and principle of the fidelity of Man to God." How gross is the misrepresentation that describes such a writer as denying the obligation of individuals to receive doctrine according to their light! Nor did he deny, but on the contrary affirmed, that in religion as well as in merely intellectual education men may with advantage receive the mere enunciations of divine truth before they have an intelligent and vital faith in the truths themselves; that the mere vehicle or formula may make way for reception of the content; that the sort of acquiescence which a young child gives to the deep doctrines of the Christian Faith prepares the mind to receive what is thus taken on trust; or rather that the spiritual truth is imperceptibly insinuated by reception of the dogmatic formula, just as in the silent teaching of nature ideas of reason and the moral being are awakened by sounds and sights, by sensuous objects and the sensuous frame of language. He well knew that every man's vital religion is as light comprehended by darkness; that it is surrounded on all sides with the indefinite, the hidden continuation of his mental horizon: but he ever protested that this introductory implicit belief is not salvation itself, but one of the ways and means of it; that the *substance* of saving faith is a beholding of divine truth; that the darkness and mystery would have no hallowing and exalting influence, if it were not the accompaniment of spiritual perceptions as *positive and sure* as the pomp of groves and garniture of fields is to the bodily eye. Mr. Coleridge's real opinions on these subjects are at equi-distance from those which the Reviewer imputes to him and those which he (the Reviewer) himself holds.

"For a Christianity founded on philosophical argument, we have not a particle of respect or value. It is a mere rope of sand, which has no principle of cohesion." A belief worthy of a reasonable man must be capable of a philosophical defence; "for no gift of God does or can contradict any other gift, except by misuse or contradiction." But Christianity must be *founded* on the testimony of the heart and spirit coinciding with the outward Revelation, not on argument and discourse of reason, metaphysical or logical. The foundation of a spiritual Religion is the same as its matter, and as a feast is founded on meat and drink, not on a deal table, so is Christianity based on its own spiritual truths and the receptivity of them in our spirit. It is the proper office of Philosophical argument to show the reasonableness of a belief so founded; to show that "the Christian religion has its objective or historic and ecclesiastic pole, and its subjective or spiritual pole: that in the miracles and miraculous parts of religion—both in the first communication of divine truths, and in the promulgation of the truths thus communicated, we have the union of the two—that is, the subjective and supernatural displayed objectively—outwardly and phenomenally—*as* subjective and supernatural." The difference betwixt Mr. Coleridge and his assailants, who seem to me like men striking passionately in the dark and hitting each other, or perhaps a dead wall, instead of the object of their enmity, is not that he founded religion on mere speculative philosophy, they on faith. They bring a philosophy to the defence of their system, as well as he to his, but he complained of this philosophy that it would not stand examination, was incompatible with philosophy at large, as taught among *philosophers,* and was only maintained in certain schools of divinity. He referred to faith as surely as they; but he maintained faith to be an act of will in the presence of reason, or a willing submission of soul to truths beheld by the Light that lighteth every man; while they seem to regard it as a blind acquiescence in the truth of something unknown. He maintained that true faith cannot be without the perception of the truth believed by the individual mind of the believer: which has been construed most unfairly—as if it meant, that there *is* no truth except that which the individual mind perceives—that is to say, no objective independent truth at all. *They* teach that faith is the bare assent to what a man is assured by authority to be true.[1] How can it benefit a man to believe that the Bible is true, without perceiving its truth? In proportion as he perceives the truth and divinity of what the Bible

[1] "Faith is the reasoning of a religious mind," says Mr. Newman, "or of what Scripture calls a right or renewed heart, which acts upon presumptions rather than evidence, which speculates and ventures when it cannot make sure of it." Faith is indeed the reasoning of a religious mind, but are not those reasonings sure in their way? Is it not *evidence, sui generis,* upon which it acts, and does it not bring a full *assurance* of the truth, when it presents to the soul the *substance* of things hoped for? Mr. Newman instances St. Paul preaching at Athens, and alleges that the evidence he gave of his message was but slight. If it had really been slight, the men who received it as *certainly* true, must have been deluded, for they could have had no spiritual insight into the truths to which they gave their assent. The saying of Locke—"The evidence that any proposition is true lying only in the proofs a man has of it, whatsoever degrees of assent he affords it beyond the degrees of that evidence, it is plain all that surplusage of assurance is owing to some other affection, and not to the love of truth," seems incontrovertible. But there is a species of evidence, the evidence of the spirit within itself, which entered not into Locke's philosophy. St. Paul, the closest of reasoners, who maintains the faith of Christ in all its parts by appealing for its truth to the higher mind of those whom he addresses, would never have expected the Athenians to believe beyond reason, or to accept aught as true of which they might not find appropriate and proportionate proof in their own hearts. Have not we good *reason* to believe the resurrection of Christ? And if *we* have reason to believe it, why must we suppose that they took for *certain* that of which they had only *presumptive* evidence? I have just perused Mr. Newman's section on the Supremacy of Faith in his *Essay on Development.* It seems to me that his general *meaning* in this disquisition would have been admitted by my Father as just, but that some of his terms and metaphysical distinctions would have been objected to.

8

contains he will believe the Bible to be divine, and a faith which out-goes this perception can be of no direct spiritual advantage to the soul. It is true that the same individual, who at one time is unable to perceive the divine character of a certain portion of Scripture, will at another time behold it as the Word of God. By use of the light that already shines within us we gain more light. But to urge this as a consideration against the argument of the "Confessions" is to mistake its drift and the author's position. The question with him turns not at all upon individual opinion respecting the internal character of passages in the Bible, but upon the value of evidence derived from this internal character in comparison with that of extrinsic proof and authority. The question with him is, whether a passage that cannot be vindicated, as to its moral bearing, by ordinary rules, founded on that law of right and wrong, which God himself has inscribed on the heart of man, is to be received as undoubtedly divine by reason of any mere external evidence that ever has been, or ever can be adduced. He never assumes that his particular view and interpretation of any portion of Scripture *must* be correct. He wrote on the Inspiration of the sacred writings in the same spirit as on other debated questions in history, politics, physics or criticism;—wrote in the sense that his judgment was fallible, his heart liable to self-deception, his moral being imperfect in the eye of God; yet considered it right, after endeavouring by all means to strengthen and purify his faculties of judgment, to state his sincere opinion. When he put forth his views on Shakespeare he wrote in the same sense of his liability to error, well aware that his opinions must fall, if they were merely individual and isolated, such as never would obtain a Catholic consent. He gave them as contributions to the dis-covery of truth, and on the same principle he put forth his views on divinity. But they who maintain against him, that such passages were given by inspiration of God, refuse to put the question on this issue. They will have it tried and decided in a different court, on different evidence, which court and witnesses he held incompetent to determine the matter ultimately and without appeal. His opponents do not them-selves affect to say that Jael's act, for instance, must not in itself appear to the common moral sense of mankind, a base, treacherous, cruel murder. But they say, "*It is in the Bible*. Deborah, an inspired person-age, extols it. Therefore we must suppose it done by divine command." Yet if we compare this bloody action of the Hebrew heroine with

Abraham's deed of truly blessed memory, how great do we find the contrast! The story of the Patriarch's intended sacrifice is evidently moral throughout. It is at once symbol and history—a striking and most affecting symbol of absolute submission to the Governor of the Universe, of perfect confidence in his goodness, as of one who orders all things for the best, and of unhesitating postponement of the transitory and perishable to the permanent invisible. The act of Jael, on the other hand, is as evidently *of the earth, earthy*; it is the act of a hard-hearted and deceitful woman, taking advantage of an open enemy by a violation of compact and of the laws of hospitality, and thus winning the gratitude of her country in the face of wickedness. It is the triumph of evil;—the wisdom of this world and its generation which seems here a higher wisdom than belongs to the children of light.

But what meant the Reviewer by affirming that Christianity, founded as he supposes Mr. Coleridge's to have been, is a mere rope of sand? Can there be no such thing as Catholic consent on internal evidence? Do men agree more absolutely on the nature and value of the outward evidences of religion, than they do on the internal consistency of the Christian scheme, on its intrinsic excellence, on its capability of fulfilling the high instincts and satisfying the needs of human nature? So far is this inward evidence from being a mere rope of sand, that it is the strong cable, bound about the faith, which has ever kept it together, and prevented the weaker bands of outward evidence from having to sustain a weight which, if it bore upon them alone, would surely break them asunder. But when writers of the Reviewer's school talk thus, are they in reality thinking of *evidence* or *mental assuredness* at all? Have they anything in their minds but the disposition and determination of certain parties to maintain whatever they have received as the truth, unaltered, whether they are able to defend it by strict argument or no? Doubtless if a set of men enter into a compact to preserve whatever they find established, without examination, there will be a wonderful concord of thought and unity of action among them. They accept a system with their eyes shut, and therefore will never be led to loosen their hold upon it from any perception of its deficiencies; for they are resolved to see nothing. The only objection to this theory of faith is, that it seems at war with the very nature of faith itself. To be determined to uphold a system is not the same thing as to feel assured that it is true and represents what is real though invisible.[1]

The doctrine which condemns private judgment labours under this difficulty, that every man must and does act on the decision of his own mind in determining whom to receive as teachers and depositories of religious truth; and since it is not possible to determine that question without judging of the truth itself, it seems a direct contradiction to say that a man may and must resolve either to embrace the system which was presented to him first by others, or to adopt another, in which he was not educated; yet that he may not reasonably judge of the system thus received. Men decide by private judgment, that the pretensions of Rome are just, and thereupon throw themselves into a communion, which denies the right of private judgment to all within its pale. For truly, so it is argued, a man may use a lantern to guide his steps through the darkness of night, and wear a heavy coat to shelter him from the inclemency of the skies out of doors; but the same

[1] I must here say, for those readers who have not yet become acquainted with the *Aids to Reflection* (what should have been said a few pages back), that Mr. Coleridge's doctrine of baptismal grace agrees with, and is, the Catholic doctrine, only not as popularly explained, or as described in the Tracts for the Times and the theological writings of Mr. Newman. His scheme establishes a more perfect analogy between the two sacraments than the other, for, according to it, Baptism gives new life to the soul, the Eucharist sustains and extends it, but both on condition of actual faith and through its operation. Both sacraments *confer* grace, which is to be appropriated by the will; why may there not be an interval of time between the consignation and the appropriation? In the holy communion as truly as in baptism, the office of the rite is only to *consign* the Holy Spirit; that the appropriation by the will should follow immediately is not essential to the doctrine; and indeed St. Augustine and other theorists on baptism have laid down, that, in certain cases, the grant does not come into operation till after an interval. But, according to the commonly received explanation of this subject, grace enters the soul in an essentially different way and with wholly different conditions in one sacrament and the other; the spirit of man is supposed to have been *born again*, the will, even after the new birth, remaining spiritually inoperative in the infant subject; and yet it is held that, in the communion, it receives benefit from the sacrament only in and with movements of life and acts of co-operation!

I have lately examined the various expressions of St. Augustine on the effect of baptism, scattered up and down his works with especial care, and am quite satisfied that he had no such thought in his mind as that of an internal spiritual renewal or change of nature in the infant soul at the font: and that his language is inconsistent with such a conception. He says, indeed, that God is with baptised little ones; but this is an ambiguous phrase, and capable of different metaphysical interpretations.

man will, of course, lay down his horn luminary, and cast aside the cumbersome frieze, when he enters a room brightly lighted by a multitude of wax candles, warmed by a brightly blazing fire, and enlivened by a gay and goodly company. And of a truth, if the faculty by which a man guides himself into a religion were analogous to the traveller's lantern—if it could be taken up and laid down again at will, and exchanged for a better means of light as soon as it had served its purpose, this supposed parallel would be very much to the point. As it is, we may fairly reply, that as it was one pair of eyes which guided the traveller to the goodly company and which enabled him to address them on his arrival; in like manner one mental organ of vision enables a man to decide respecting the Church, and to examine the doctrines which are said to be taught by the Church. It is urged against this view that men choose their own physicians and lawyers without pretending to judge of the prescriptions of the former, or to criticise the legal opinions of the latter. But neither case is really in point. In the practical matters that concern the present life a man is obliged to act upon uncertainties; he acts for the best, but with the consciousness that he may fail. He is obliged to choose his physician or lawyer by common report, and he often chooses wrong. Still if he happens to choose right, he derives full benefit from his choice though he neither understands physic nor law. Religion is not like material medicine or the business of the lawyer, a thing by which a man may be benefited irrespectively of any personal knowledge or understanding of it in its internal character. To choose a religion is to feel *sure* that it is true, and to secure its blessings is to embrace with our whole heart and mind and spirit its saving truths, and enlightening, purifying revelations. I believe that my father had as high a respect for a real Catholic consent or an uninterrupted tradition as most men; but he was too independent and brave, too reflective and clear-minded, to bow down before the idol of Public Opinion; to adopt vulgar conservative maxims, and yield to the despotism of a mere existing majority.

To this Existing Majority the English Reviewer appeals in mean-minded triumph: one of the many proofs his disquisition affords, that he can have no confidence in the intrinsic merits of his cause. "These men fear public opinion," says he: "They know that the national mind of England is strongly adverse to their views. They know the principles of the clergy as a body, and they are fearful of provoking a strong re-action." This is an appeal to the violent and unthinking Many against the Few, whose opinions are too refined to be popular on their first promulgation. They who dwell in the dark are ever ready to behold objects of terror, fiends and goblins on all sides round, as soon as their imaginations are excited by fearful picturings and cries of alarm: on this propensity the Reviewer seems to calculate in his procedure. He would make the writers whom he assails objects of apprehension; and as

> "Fear and Rage are one disease—
> And both alike the ague,"

this was well devised to bring upon them the anger of that numerous class whose zeal is not according to knowledge; but in ascribing fear of public opinion to *them*, and accusing them of "miserable party spirit," he is as wide of the mark of truth as in all his other arrow shots. The temper of fearlessness and moral courage is the natural companion of free inquiry, and it is a fact that most of the men of whom the writer speaks thus are eminently bold and incautious. The timid and self-preservative are ever desirous of belonging to a party in whose ranks they may be hidden; by whose many weapons they may be protected. Where there is a tacit compact amongst any set of men, that they shall *act* as one even while they *think* diversely, each sacrificing something that is dear to him, like the triumvirs of old, in order to secure the help of the rest towards acquiring or preserving something still dearer and more important, there is party spirit. Party coalitions in this corrupt and evil sense cannot be for those who hold it the duty of each individual to follow the light which presents itself, or seems to present itself, to his individual mind, and who permit no bond of union except the common perception of truth.

Achilles pursued one whom he took to be a mere man beside the deep-eddying Scamander, and ever and anon he thought to overtake him with his swift feet and overpower him with his potent arm. But after a while the supposed Agenor turned about and confronted him, and began to remonstrate seriously with the pride-blinded hero on the vanity of his endeavours; and behold it was no mere man, weak, mortal, vanquishable; but a god, even the god Apollo, strong, deathless, unconquerable, full of light and full of might.[1] So in the strength of vaunted systems of outward evidence, unqualified submission to authority, passive acquiescence and logic apart from metaphysic insight, many a vain boaster will pursue beside the loud stream of Public Opinion, that Christian Philosophy, whereof there are now so many vigorous youthful champions, and of which Coleridge, were he alive at this day, would be a veteran defender. But methinks they will find, when they fancy themselves about to seize and overthrow the object of their hostility, that it is no mere shadowy, baseless German-ism, has nothing in common with that shallow Rationalism of the old unspiritual Unitarian system, which, now superannuated and in the last stage of decay, receives a sort of contemptuous protection, in consideration that it is not long for this world, from a bold-faced, hollow-hearted son and heir, called Esoteric or Idealised Christianity, who describes the Gospel as a well feigned tale devised for the edifica-tion of the people—a mortal Minerva, sprung not from Jove, but from the head of mere humanity. Methinks they will find it strong and imperishable, divine on both sides, as embracing an outward revelation, that has come down from heaven, and an inward revelation of the Spirit bearing witness to our spirit, which is the work of God in the soul of man.

That these Letters on inspiration fully and unobjectionably solve the whole difficult problem of the Bible, in what sense as to particulars, as well as considered at large, it is the Word of God, I cannot pretend to say. But of this I feel assured, that the work is a step in the right direction, and tends to reflection upon the insufficiency, the indefinite-ness, or self-contradictoriness of the popular scheme, if scheme *that* can be called, which certain settled form has none; and indicates, as far as it goes, the true principles, on which the subject ought to be examined. Of this also I feel assured, that many of the objections hither-to brought against it, are made in ignorance or prejudice,—misappre-hension of the main drift of the work, with inversion of some of its

---

[1] Τίπτε με, Πηλέος υἷε, ποσὶν ταχέεσσι διώκεις,
αὐτὸς θνητὸς ἐὼν θεὸν ἄμβροτον ; οὐδέ νύ πώ με
ἔγνως, ὡς θεός εἰμι, σὺ δ ἀσπερχὲς μενεαίνεις.

. . . .

οὐ μέν με κτενέεις, ἐπεὶ οὔτοι μόρσιμός εἰμι.

arguments, and peremptory assertions concerning the sense of passages in Holy Writ, supposed, as thus understood, to overthrow the doctrine of the treatise.

Some defenders of Plenary Inspiration insist that in the "Confessions" my father fights with a shadow, an imaginary combatant of his own devising. I do not speak confidently on this deep and arduous theme: but I own it is a question with me whether they who talk thus have ever subjected their own notions to metaphysical analysis, or have beheld them in that clear keen light of mental science, in which Mr. Coleridge was accustomed to contemplate all theological propositions and schemes of doctrine addressed to the speculative faculty. I cannot help inferring from the remarks of these objectors both in negativing my father's statements, and positively asserting the view they substitute, that their scheme *is*, in substance and real *value*, tantamount to that which, as exhibited in these pages, appears to them a mere shadow; that it *does*, in fact, involve that mere mechanical dictation, which they mean to reject: that it is either this or nothing. Of such schemes my father plainly confessed—"I cannot understand them." For do not all the maintainers of *theopneusty*,—as maintainers of plenary inspiration now call themselves, though the term certainly does not etymologically exclude my father's view,—do not all the adversaries of the scheme which my father proposed as really better, safer, more truly satisfying to the heart and higher mind than any other which has yet been formally stated, eagerly contend, that both in regard to doctrine and moral sentiment, and in regard to facts of history, the Sacred Writers were infallibly guided so that they could not err? Is it conceivable that any human mind should be free to use its own powers, express its own feelings, record its own experience, while it is so divinely controlled as to be kept from all possibility of error? Is infallibility possible except in the case of divine *information* superseding all the native powers and acquired abilities of the mortal penman, all his personal emotions, reflections, and imaginations? The faithful have light from heaven shining in upon their human mind through reason the *power* of divine light in the soul. In so far as any Christian is regenerate his human will is strengthened and sustained by the Holy Spirit. But in this case there is no infallibility,—no exemption from the *possibility* of error in thought, —of faultiness in act and deed. By the reasoners to whom I allude not only are the sacred historians pronounced infallible—the personages whom they describe as carrying forward the designs of God are declared sacred too, even where no comment is made upon their action in the holy record. Ehud, Jael, David, for all his acts except those which are expressly blamed, are held up to honour or sheltered from blame. To such a scheme we may well apply the description of my father; we may well say of *it* what he said of the supposed *imaginary* doctrine, that it "petrifies at once the whole body of Holy Writ with all its harmonies and symmetrical gradations"—"evacuates of *all sense and efficacy* the sure and constant tradition, that all the several books bound up together in our precious family Bibles were composed in different and widely distant ages, &c." Thus at least I think we must regard it, if we attempt to place it before us in any definite consistent form. If it be not a scheme of divine information, superseding the individual mind, how is it to be understood?

My father's objections to the doctrine of Plenary Inspiration as applied to the book of Job have been treated as evincing an ignorance of the manner in which it is held by competent defenders. Who has the folly, they say, to suppose, that in an inspired narrative the speeches of every speaker must be divine *truth*? They do not seem to ask *themselves* the question, Are the speeches of Job's friends true and faithful expressions of human thoughts and feelings, or are they not? If they are such, why must we ascribe them to the infinite and eternal Being as their author? If my father imagined that the speeches of Bildad, Eliphaz, and Zophar were conceived by *all* maintainers of plenary inspiration to convey religious truth, I should believe him wrong. But this does not affect his argument in its main drift. Is it not undeniable that his opponents represent them as having flowed from no human heart, but from the Spirit of Truth, informing the sacred writer what to record? Of this view he said that it took away all sympathy and all example.

In the same spirit objectors have said: "Mr. Coleridge is carried away by imagination and spends his eloquence in declaiming against absurdities of his own inventing. He knows neither what he means himself, nor what they mean whom he opposes. Who ever supposed that David was an automaton poet, mourner and supplicant? Of course he recorded his own experiences, his own feelings: but the record was so overruled that it became a full, perfect, and particular prophecy of the Messiah." I confess this mode of defending Plenary Inspiration looks to me very like Charles Stuart's defence of his trusty servant Strafford,—"faithful friend" that he was!—that is to say an abandonment of it to its fate. If David expressed his own feelings, related his own troubles, hopes and fears, joys and sorrows, perils, and deliverances, how can it be affirmed that his mind was infallibly guided or that the record in all its parts was the work of inspiration? Can it be thought that the Holy Ghost did that which the man David was able by human means to do himself? And is it maintained that any record of human thoughts and feelings will be free from the leaven of human infirmity? How can a reasoner who admits that David wrote as a man might write, mourned as a man might mourn, and uttered such strains of poetry as man might compose, maintain the plenary inspiration of Holy Writ in the sense objected to by my father? That the events of David's life, his composition of the Psalms included, were so ordered by Providence that the whole was typical and prophetic of our Lord and Saviour, this is just what my father would have insisted on, and is a way of viewing the subject perfectly consonant with his whole conception of the divine dealings with man, of the Inspiration of Scripture, and of the grand plan of divine government from the beginning of the world. If there are others who are disposed to join in this charge that the author of the Confessions fights against a shadow, let them read Dr. Whitby's General Preface on Inspiration of Scripture, and I think they will find the shadow to be a very substantial body— no dead body as yet, though perhaps in the way to become so. Let them remember too that he anticipates this very objection at the beginning of Letter IV. "Let nothings count for nothing, and the dead bury the dead! Who but such ever understood the Tenet in this sense?"— "In what sense then do others understand it? What other sense is conceivable that does not *destroy the doctrine which it proposes to interpret?*"

But my father's view is decried as *unsafe*. What security have we for any part of the faith in Christ, if any part of what is contained in the Canon may be human error rather than divine truth? We may ask in reply, what security can we have that faith is a genuine insight, a saving assuredness of divine truth, if such an external, superficial security as this is indispensable? Such a security as this my father held most dangerous to the interests of true religion: it is a security like that of mandragora, which allays the heat of fever by making the patient sleep to death.

I could not of course enter here into a general defence of the treatise, even if I were prepared and competent to the task; but I will notice two instances in which it has been charged with obvious error, on the mere assumption that certain interpretations of Scripture, by no means universally adopted amongst noted divines, are unquestionably right. At page 59 the author cites, among other passages which he conceives it not necessary to accept as the very word of God, *Acts* vii. 53.—*Gal.* iii. 19. (*Heb.* ii. 2. *may* refer to the same thing or it may not.) This ordination or delivery of the Law by Angels, which my father looked upon as a piece of human tradition, like that of Michael's dispute with the Devil about the body of Moses, mentioned by St. Jude, is solemnly declared to have been pre-announced in *Psalm* lxviii. 17—that is to say, a mere conjecture of *some* commentators is relied on as if it were the sentence of a sovereign inappellable authority, or were supported by a true Catholic consent. The Psalmist only tells us that the Lord rode upon Cherubim as in a triumphal chariot, and that in this sublime equipage he descended on Mount Sinai. The ordination of the Law by Angels is something quite different from the attendance of Angels upon the Lord, or their serving him as a chariot. To identify the one with the other is most arbitrary—a sample of the violent proceedings of Bible critics, who *must* furnish some sort of explanation of every difficult passage in Scripture in accordance with the dogmatism of their school. To convey the Lord to Sinai—is to ordain the law at Sinai—or implies it!

So again, the Angel of the Lord, who called upon the Israelites to curse bitterly the inhabitants of Meroz, as we read in the Song of Deborah, is declared in the same undoubting way to be none other than our blessed Lord Himself: and on the strength of this identification the curse is reckoned among those parts of Holy Scripture, specified at p. 44, which are referred by the sacred penman to a direct communication from God! Surely it is far safer, more consonant with the tenor of the passage and with a reasonable view of the whole subject, if we take this Angel of the Lord, as some learned divines have done, for Barak, the executor of divine wrath; and it will hardly be maintained by any considerate person, that the Almighty always executes his wrath by divine or even by holy instruments. The vengeance of the Lord may come, yet wrath be upon those by whom it comes.[1]

[1] I have lately perused an interesting manuscript commenting on the

Can the maintainers of such views as those here objected to, be sure that they are really honourable to the Father of Lights—really fitted to inspire and confirm that abiding sense and untheorising perception of the supreme goodness and wisdom of God, which is the deepest ground of belief in Him and fealty toward Him, as our personal Liege Lord, and the Moral Governor of the world? Can they be sure that the horror with which they receive any suggestion to the contrary does not proceed from attachment to a particular theory concerning the Bible, which they have been taught to identify with religion,—an attachment that has its seat in the fancy and understanding, rather than from genuine zeal for the stability of faith in the Holy Spirit, and pious jealousy lest any belief, conducive to the shining forth of his glory in the hearts and minds of his rational creatures, should be under-mined?

I shall cite in conclusion Adam Clarke's observation on the event recorded in the fifth chapter of Judges. This will serve to show that intelligent persons who believe, or think they believe, the popular doctrine of plenary inspiration have been unable to carry out such a belief consistently, or to accept in good earnest the servile bibliolatry, which maintains the *moral* blessedness of Jael, and insists on exalting her as a heroine-saint, actuated by the Spirit of holiness, a type of the meek mother of our merciful Redeemer.

After reciting the circumstances of the assassination under ten heads, he proceeds to say. "Now do we not find in all this, bad faith, deceit, deep hypocrisy, lying, breach of treaty, contempt of religious rites, breach of the laws of hospitality, deliberate and unprovoked murder? But what can be said in her justification? All that can be said, and all that has been said, is simply this: 'She might have been sincere at first, but was afterwards divinely directed to do what she did.' If this

Confessions of an Inquiring Spirit, written by a decided dissentient from the views of the author, but a fair and straight-forward one, who sometimes, I *think*, mistakes the true import of those views, but never wilfully misrepresents them. This critique is written in so good a spirit, shows so much acuteness and know-ledge of Scripture, and enters upon the examination of my father's little work in so elaborate and legitimate a manner, that I cannot help wishing the author would revise and publish it. I have no stronger desire with regard to the Letters on Inspiration than that they should be subjected to close and searching *honest* criticism. A trial not fairly conducted can but throw darkness on the face of the subject.—Truth was never yet advanced by untruthful methods, except indirectly in the discussion which those Popish practices may lead to.

was so, she is sufficiently vindicated by the fact; for God has a right to dispose of the lives of his creatures as he pleases: and probably the cup of Sisera's iniquity was full, and his life already forfeited to the justice of God. But does it appear that she received any such direction from God? There is no sufficient evidence of it: it is true that Deborah, a prophetess, declares her *blessed above women*; and this seems to intimate that her conduct was pleasing to God. If Deborah was inspired on this occasion, her words are a presumptive proof that the act was right; unless we are to understand it as a simple declaration of the reputation she should be held in among her own sex.[1] But we do not find one word from Jael herself, stating how she was led to do an act repugnant to her feelings as a woman, contrary to good faith, and a breach of the rules of hospitality. Nor does the sacred penman say one word to explain the case; as in the case of Ehud, he states the fact, and leaves his readers to form their own opinion."

"To say as has been said in the case of *Eglon*, that 'Sisera was a *public enemy*, and any of the people whom he oppressed might be justified in taking away his life,' is a very dangerous position, as it refers one of the most solemn acts of judgment and justice to the caprice, or prejudice, or enthusiastic feeling of every individual who may persuade himself, that he is not only concerned in the business, but authorised by God to take vengeance by his own hand. While justice and law are in the world, God never will, as he never did, abandon cases of this kind to the caprice, prejudice, or party feeling of any man. The conduct of Ehud and Jael are before the tribunal of God: I will not justify, I dare not absolutely condemn; there I leave them, and entreat my readers to do the like."

Honest Adam, this cannot be: if you wished your readers to form no judgment on the case, you should not have gone so far in attempting to direct their judgment. Upon such a survey the mind involuntarily passes sentence on the deed, *as presented to us in the Bible narrative.* Jael *herself* is before the tribunal of God, and we dare not determine what his decision has been on any human being rendering the last account—

[1] On verse 24 of the following chapter (*Judges*, chap. v) Adam Clarke has the following note: "*Blessed* above women shall Jael be. She shall be highly celebrated as a most heroic woman; all the Israelitish women shall glory in her. I do not understand these words as expressive of the divine approbation towards Jael.— The word *bless*, both in *Hebrew* and *Greek*, often signifies *to praise, to speak well of, to celebrate.* This is most probably the sense here."

no not even in the instance of Judas; but the Jael of *Judges* our heart and our reason cannot but condemn.

S. C.

N.B.—I feel assured that a passage, left without an explanatory sentence, through the inadvertence of haste, will be taken by the candid reader in the spirit in which it was conceived. It will not be supposed that, in that passage, any parallel, however slight or partial, between a fallible human being and the sinless Saviour of mankind was insinuated, or that anything more was meant than an illustration, such as might reverently be made,—a comparison not of persons, but remotely of situation and circumstance.

S. C.

EXTRACT FROM A LETTER
FROM COLERIDGE TO MR. HESSEY

Extract from a letter of 23 May 1825 from Coleridge to Mr. Hessey, reprinted, by permission of the publishers, from E. L. Griggs, *Unpublished Letters of Samuel Taylor Coleridge,* London, Constable & Co., Ltd., 1932, vol. 2, Letter 352:

MY DEAR SIR,

Since I left you, I have been *moiling* for an Appropriate and inviting Title for, and instead of, the Six Disquisitions. A late Physiologist represents the nervous System as a Plant, of which the Spinal Cord, is the stem and the Brain the compound Flower—and if you have ever watched a Humble bee at a Fox-glove or a Monkshood, visiting one Bell after another, and bustling and humming in each, you will have no bad likeness of the dips and dives I have been making into the several cells and campanula of my Brain. Two, only have occurred to me, or rather the same in two forms, both suggested by real incidents—the first, Conversations on Stainmoor (n.b. the dreariest and longest Waste-land in England) the second.—The young Chaplain and the Grey-headed Passenger: or Conversations on Shipboard—or Convers. during a Voyage to the Mediterranean—or Cabin Conversations on subjects of moral and religious interest—Supplemental of the *Aids to Reflection* or lastly thus—
The grey-headed Passenger: or Conversations on Shipboard during a voyage to the Mediterranean, supplemental of the *Aids to Reflection* by S. T. Coleridge.
My supposed fellow-passenger a young Clergyman, newly ordained who had subscribed the 39 Articles on the principles of Paley as mere Articles of Peace, quite satisfied in conscience that he should never preach counter to them as he should never trouble himself or his flock about them. He should keep to the *Morality* of the Gospel and simply teach his Hearers to do as they would be done by. In short, his Divinity would consist of two chapters—first—that Honesty is the best Policy; and second, if you don't find it so here, you will hereafter. But notwithstanding this very compendious, convenient and portable faith, I find him a young man of fine intellect, and generous feelings, a good classic, an enthusiastic lover of Nature etc. The Conversations are supposed to take place during the latter half of the Voyage—The first indeed at Gibraltar —and to have been preceeded by a long series of discussions, which had ended in convincing him of the hollowness of the ground on which he had hitherto stood, of the cheerlessness, vulgarity and common-place character of the Mechanical philosophy and Paleyian Expedience—but still more in impressing him with the superior *power* and ampler *Command* given by the habit of seeking for the first principles of all living and effective truth in the constitution and constituent faculties of the Mind itself. He is roused and affected by an

animated portraiture of the Life and Labors of a Minister of the Gospel, who is at the same time a Philosopher and a Christian and who finds the consummation and most perfect form of Philosophy in Christianity—and declares his determination to set about the building up of the philosophic mind in himself— but is mortified by the doubts which the grey-headed Passenger expresses as to his perseverance in the task—and in the irritation occasioned by this unexpected Check avows his contempt and detestation of all quackery and mystery, and asks indignantly—If this Philosophy be true and important and agreeable to the Reason, Moral Being, and all the contra-distinguishing Attributes of Humanity, what should make it of such difficult acquirement for any man of education, and tolerable strength of intellect? And with the answer to this question the Conversations commence; and after the two first that he begins to read the Aids to Reflection.

What is your judgement of this as a Title, and as the *Mould* of the Work? . . .

A